GOVERNMENT RUINS
Nearly EVERYTHING

Government Ruins *nearly* Everything

Reclaiming Social Issues From Uncivil Servants

———————

Laura Carno

ISBNs: 978-0692672754 (paperback)

Printed in the United States of America
First Printing: 2016
20   19   18   17   16   5   4   3   2   1

Cover and interior design by Ryan Scheife/Mayfly Design

Created Equal Publishing
To order, visit www.lauracarno.com

To my husband Bill, for going on this adventure with me.

ACKNOWLEDGMENTS

This book started with an idea: that people are best equipped to make the decisions that govern their lives, and that when government butts its nose in, *bad things always happen*. Regardless of the side of the aisle you find yourself on, or which side of the aisle an issue finds itself on, this principle applies. Government ruins nearly everything it touches.

This book wouldn't have happened without a lot of people pushing, cajoling, nudging, and prodding me. If not for them, the ideas in this book would still be floating in space, hanging separately without the threads that bind them into one unified political philosophy.

Many people never knew they were participating in book research, yet nonetheless helped me recognize the universal need for people to make their own decisions. They are the ones whose patience never flagged in the face of my many questions, or my endless "tell me more about how you learned that," follow-ups.

Although many people took their valuable time to educate me on a particular issue, I would like to specifically thank some people who shared in this venture as if it were their own.

First, thanks to my parents, who taught me—beginning in the 1960s—that I could do anything I wanted to do.

Thank you to my friend and editor Glenn Miller, who acted as guide and mentor. He encouraged me to put these ideas into print, and challenged me to question what I thought I knew. He also helped me to more clearly describe how the threads of political philosophy are all bound together on principled foundations. Glenn's talent for finding the single word to convey what took me four or five—or a whole sentence—is impressive.

Thank you to Alex Chaffetz, who helped me find my political voice. He encouraged me to use my natural manner of speaking to relate to voters in a persuasive way. Without his guidance, I would not have considered communicating on TV and radio.

Thank you to Shari Williams, who helped to ground me in principle, understand how to argue from those principles, and get past my comfort zone. Her Leadership Program of the Rockies experience was a game changer for my career path.

Thank you to my fellow authors John Daly, Kevin Sayles, and Cam Edwards, who were generous with their time in coaching me through writing a book.

And finally, thank you to my non-political husband Bill, for tolerating the peculiar dinner table conversations and for entertaining my questions that started with, "As a normal person, what do you think of..."

Contents

THIS IS FOR YOUR OWN GOOD!

As children we were told to eat our vegetables and wait an hour before swimming. Facing our disgruntled scowls, every parent echoed the same refrain: "This is for your own good!"

When young, we needed the guidance. What to eat. When to sleep. Where to ride our bikes. How soon to send a thank you note to Auntie and Uncle for the lovely Christmas sweater.

Thanks, folks—for all the necessary values that only you could provide. But we're grown up now.

Those parental lessons mattered; they worked. But now there's an overbearing parent-by-proxy for all of us, and it's ruining nearly everything.

Sure, government put a man on the moon. It generally defends our rights and sometimes even our borders. But it also fails spectacularly to spend within its means, let businesses thrive, and solve social problems that it claims to be able to fix. Most of all it fails to stay out of where it doesn't belong—the millions of minor acts and choices that make up the daily lives of ostensibly free citizens.

Eighteen-year-olds who imagine that being commanded and constrained ends when they move out discover too soon that government is a lot bossier than mom and dad.

There isn't much the government doesn't control when the average American starts her day, from the prescribed water flow in toilets and showers, to the mandated nutrition labeling on a box of breakfast cereal, to the warning label forever sealed to the cord of her blow-dryer. The government also tells her what type of light bulb she may buy, which features her car must have, and whether it is legal to collect rainwater that falls on her own roof.

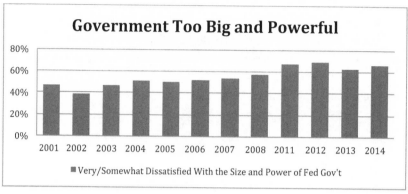

Government Too Big and Powerful

■ Very/Somewhat Dissatisfied With the Size and Power of Fed Gov't

Source: Gallup Poll, 2001-2014

Do any of these requirements, any of these mandates, make our lives better?

Bureaucrats tell us that these decisions are for our own good. They keep us healthy and safe, and protect the environment. Bureaucrats tell us, *and sometimes we believe them*, that they know what's best for us. So the government, under both major political parties, drowns us in best intentions with laws that keep us from living freely.

All because they know best. How foolish it would be to actually trust citizens. Much better to control them.

---

*No government that trusts you mandates
what you must do "for your own good."*

It's no wonder that two-thirds of Americans told Gallup in January 2014 that government is too big and powerful.

But the elected officials aren't the only ones at fault.

Voters, both Democrat and Republican, continue to elect people—at every level—who make government more intrusive in our day-to-day lives. Whether on traditionally conservative issues like abortion and marriage, or traditionally liberal issues like guns and education, both sides find ways to multiply regulations, pile on prohibitions, and plain old meddle more.

Why do we keep asking government officials to fix our problems and expect that they can? We keep thinking that just this once they might do it right. Just this once they will have our best interests at heart. Just this once they will fix the evils. Just. This. Once.

Our country *does* have big problems to solve. But the only time government makes things better is when it does nothing, letting the people who actually care about the problems fix them voluntarily.

This predicament is most acute on social issues. How is the government, composed of people who happen to have been elected, any better equipped to make decisions than unelected individuals?

It isn't.

Government isn't smarter than you.

Despite being no better qualified than private citizens, bureaucrats have one thing the rest of us don't: the power to tell us what to do.

That power is misused and misplaced, especially when government can't get its own house in order. Especially when its "fixes" so often make problems worse. War on poverty? More poverty. War on drugs? No better.

So why, especially on the issues dearest to us—love and marriage, equality and education, self-protection and the sanctity of life—would we cede control to the government?

Abdicating personal responsibility is no part of being a mature adult.

We are perfectly capable of making our own decisions, both the mundane and the complex ones. After all, it is *our own* life, health, and safety in question. Having decision-making capability, it is our obligation to run our own lives and solve our own problems. Surrendering these responsibilities to the government is reckless and lazy.

Besides, I trust citizens like you and me, ordinary people acting as they deem best, to be more committed and more effective than any collection of imperious government officials.

So Many Nosy Neighbors

Republican or Democrat, government busybodies act like our nosy neighbor who, if she were as meddling as they are, would surely be told to mind her own business. Picture her peeking in your windows, wagging her finger with disapproval. Maybe she thinks you are feeding your children improperly, watching the wrong TV shows, or turning your thermostat up too high. We wouldn't tolerate this behavior from a neighbor, so why do we put up with it from government?

I once sat in on a card game with some elderly relatives who lived in a neighborhood with mostly retired seniors like themselves. Nearly all of the conversation was about the other neighbors. Everyone knew who had visitors and where they were from. Everyone knew the latest on everyone else's medical procedures. One player even *tsked* at a slightly scandalous magazine seen in a neighbor's shopping cart at the grocery store.

This sounds like many government agencies. Lacking enough productive work, they scrutinize everything *we* are doing, then concoct rules to limit our activities. You know who doesn't have time to be nosy? Someone getting real work done—which is to say, not most of our government!

Most of us willingly accept some government interference. Americans generally agree that traffic lights are a good idea, for example, despite their momentary intrusions into our schedules. Those lights increase public safety, with little downside. We also likely agree on certain limits, where interference becomes overreach. A government agency shutting down a kid's lemonade stand is going too far, most of us acknowledge. Such innocent industriousness and enterprise don't merit government meddling.

And yet, when facing the most important issues our country must solve, we ask the government to nose in and micromanage our lives. Why do we think this way? Why do we shirk the responsibility to solve our own problems?

For our pet causes, we paradoxically want to carve out an exception to our usual maxim that "government is too controlling," creating this baffling conundrum:

We don't want the government butting in,
unless it's our kind of butting in.

We don't hear anyone, Republican or Democrat, say that too much government is always a bad thing. Neither major party consistently says that government should stay out of our lives, *regardless of the issue*. But two-thirds of Americans still think the government is too big and too powerful.

This is philosophical inconsistency of the highest order, when we imagine that government knows best, but only for issues we want to use its power of force to impose.

Privileges in Portions

In the United States we are a nation of citizens, not subjects. The difference between the two is that as citizens, we are the ones with the rights. But today, government's current overreaches have skewed this dynamic, and numbed us to an inexorable and overbearing erosion of those rights.

"All Men Are Created Equal" means that I—the citizen—am created equal to any government official. No smug administrator is the boss of me. No petty bureaucrat, even if well-meaning, has the moral authority to tell me what to do. It's not their job to tell us how to live, or to intrude on the hundreds of micro-decisions we make every day.

But today, the government does all of that and much more. According to *Ten Thousand Commandments*, the Competitive Enterprise Institute's annual survey of the federal regulatory state, 1.43 million pages have been added to the *Federal Register* in the past 20 years. That daily government publication issues proposed and final administrative regulations of federal agencies.

Are there 1.43 million pages of things wrong in our country?

Do we really think the government can and should fix them?

And for all of those regulations, are we better off? Has the government actually fixed anything, or has this excess perverted the founders' intent? Our Constitution was adopted to constrain government, not to sustain those decisions that over-reaching politicians would like to make for us.

We do not live in a country where we wait for the government to deliver privileges to us in small portions as it sees fit. This relationship between us citizens and *our* government is out of balance. As Americans, we are free men and free women who live in a country whose documents restrain the government, even if too many of us have lost sight of that.

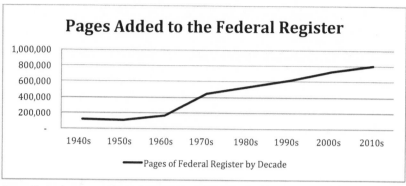

Source: National Archives and Records Administration, Office of the Federal Register

The Fix Is In

Politicians make big promises. End world hunger. Give power back to the people. Fix income inequality. End corporate welfare. Cure cancer. Save the children.

But there's a problem.

Most government solutions fix nothing.

Poverty plagues most of our nation, especially in large urban centers, despite the War on Poverty. The illicit drug addiction rate has remained stagnant since 1970, despite the War on Drugs. Medical and college costs soar, despite Obamacare and federalized student loans. Farms and industries fail, despite protectionism and subsidies. All while the federal debt grows beyond historic limits.

When politicians set lofty goals, but then enact policies that undermine those goals, citizens should be very suspicious. Again and again politicians push for fixes that have been proven *not* to work, and ask us to trust in a different result. We didn't spend enough money, they say. We didn't regulate tightly enough. We didn't control the populace enough. People weren't selfless enough.

I say, "Enough!"

Government isn't fixing the problems because government *can't* fix the problems. Not when they abuse their authority, operate with the wrong incentives, and view their citizens as complicit drones.

Why should one government solution for a particular problem be the only effective one? Isn't it more likely that thousands of adequate solutions exist nationwide, to solve thousands of problems nationwide, in thousands of private-interaction laboratories nationwide? Why do we continue to tolerate one-size-fits-all solutions in a no-size-fits-all country?

Freedom Is Hard Work

It is easy to advocate personal freedom; we trust ourselves implicitly. It is much harder to support freedom for everyone else, especially if we don't approve of how they express it.

Some people find it difficult to advocate for freedoms they don't like. Consider a gun-control activist who is also a proponent of same-sex marriage. Can this activist do the hard work of equating the freedom to choose your own self-defense with the freedom to choose your own life partner, and acknowledge that the freedom to own guns and the freedom of same-sex couples to marry are both expressions of the same principle?

Freedom can make us uncomfortable. Fully embracing it means supporting how other people express their freedoms, even when those expressions conflict with our own deeply held personal values or religious beliefs. It means recognizing that freedom is a principle bigger than any one issue. For our activist it means making peace with the notion that to be allowed the freedom to live her way, she must grant freedom to others to do the same.

Everyone's freedom is important, because freedom itself is important.

Abraham Lincoln understood that when he said, "Those who deny freedom to others deserve it not for themselves." So did Gandhi: "I'm a lover of my own liberty, and so I would do nothing to restrict yours."

I like the expression, "Utopia is not an option." There will never be a perfect utopian society, where everyone lives as *you* would like. But there is another utopia where everyone lives as *they* would like. And as long as what *they* like doesn't impose on our lives, there's room for all of us to be just fine with that.

WHO DESERVES YOUR TRUST?

Trust is sacred.

It's earned, not given, and when properly bestowed, trust encourages closeness, distributes responsibility, and smoothes transactions. Yet when it's misplaced, the result is betrayal.

With private citizens we have remedies for violations of trust—private sanctions and future avoidance among them. When government and its bureaucrats abuse the same trust—what then?

The question is: Who has earned your trust and who has a history of abusing or betraying it?

Fireworks

There are many things "wrong" with our country that people would like to see "fixed," but among them, four social issues generate the most fireworks:

- Abortion
- Guns
- Schools
- Same-sex marriage

These attract massive political dollars and incite riotous political noise. Hundreds of millions of lobbying dollars have been spent to either restrict or enhance freedoms, to control outcomes or to create choice, or to urge the government to "fix" whatever the problem is.

For such incendiary issues, is it better to leave a fix to the government, or to trust the citizens for answers?

These issues matter. They are personal and profound—deeply heartfelt, often faith-based, and with life-altering consequences. So why should we turn them over to bureaucrats to handle? Have they earned our trust? Is the government even capable of fixing such big problems?

Many use these Fireworks issues to insist that governmental intervention is the only way to create equitable outcomes or sound societal norms. What's lost in these arguments is the fundamental concept that an individual's stance on such issues often turns on very complex and highly variable personal moral and philosophical underpinnings. This is ground the "policy boot" of government is ill-equipped to dance through. Looking at politicians' records on these issues, however, helps us question the consistency of both major political parties and challenge their claims of wanting less government intervention in our personal lives.

Inevitability

Increasingly, Americans want more control over their own lives, especially for these Fireworks issues.

Parents want more control over their children's education, so they consider options other than traditional neighborhood schools.

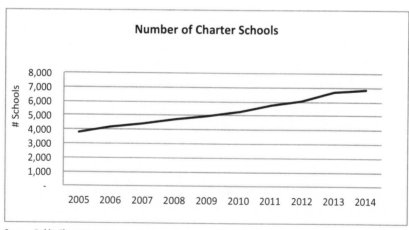

Source: *PublicCharters.org*

Although more Americans think of themselves as pro-life on abortion, they don't think the way to reduce the incidence of abortion is for the government to make it illegal.

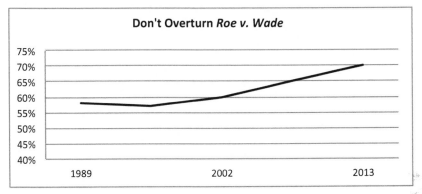

Source: Gallup Poll, 2013

Regardless of what people think of the morality of same-sex marriage, they approve of its legality.

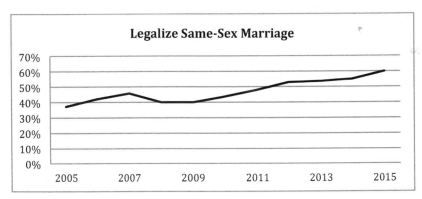

Source: Gallup Poll, 2015

Americans are increasingly more likely to believe that restricting gun ownership is not the way to reduce gun violence.

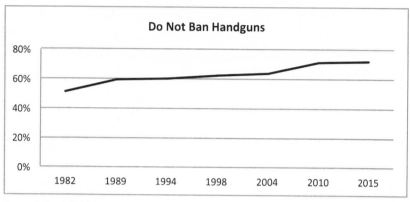

Do Not Ban Handguns

Source: *Gallup Poll, 2015*

These trends don't mirror the traditional left-right political thinking. They are based instead on the growing understanding that we citizens—not the government—know best how to live our own lives.

Our country is favoring school choice, individual gun rights, a woman's access to a legal abortion, and anyone's right to marry. These four trends coincide. They suggest inevitability. And they're generational.

Millennials, those born in the 1980s or 1990s, whether liberal or conservative, are generally in favor of more individual choice and less government control on all of these Fireworks issues. According to a Harvard University study on millennial attitudes toward government, 74% don't trust the federal government to do the right thing, and 63% don't trust the President to do the right thing.

This doesn't mean that millennials favor abortions, gun crime, underperforming schools, and crumbling marriages. It means that they are accustomed to solving their own problems, that they don't view the government as a universal cure-all.

Millennials are the iPhone generation. They solve problems with a small miracle in the palm of their hands. When they need to define a word, they Google it. When they need to choose a restaurant, they Yelp it. Cab ride? Uber. New desk? Craigslist.

These policy-makers of tomorrow trust themselves, their technology, and especially their peers in our connected economy to solve their own problems.

For the Fireworks issues it's no different. Private solutions, not intrusive government policies, are making the most impact and, where fixes are needed, the best answers come from putting trust in individuals, not in the government.

Government Is Broken

Trusting individuals to solve important issues is practical, especially because government doesn't fix much of anything. In *Why Government Doesn't Work*, Harry Browne, the 2000 Libertarian Party Presidential candidate, describes it best:

> The decline of America has been caused by politicians and reformers who believe that you aren't competent to run your own life, that they know better how to spend the money you've earned, that they understand which products you should be allowed to buy and what wages and job benefits are suitable for you.
>
> To run your life for you, they have created a government that fails at everything it undertakes, but wants to undertake everything:
>
> The government can't deliver the mail on time, but wants to take your life in its hands by controlling your health care.
>
> The government can't keep the peace in Washington, D.C., but it sends troops on "peacekeeping missions" to Somalia and Haiti—to save those countries from being run by the wrong thugs.
>
> Government schools don't have the money and time to teach your children how to read well—yet they always find the resources to teach their favorite social theories, no matter how distressing they are to parents.
>
> Wherever we look, government fails at what we want, and succeeds only in finding new ways to interfere with our lives.

Browne wrote this in 1995, but it could just as well have been written today. The same problems have plagued us for decades, and the government is not equipped to fix them. If it could, Browne's words wouldn't sound current or familiar.

You're Not the Boss of Me

If government doesn't work, then where do we draw the line between those things we decide for ourselves and those things we allow the government—elected officials and unelected bureaucrats alike—to decide for us?

At work, our boss has the authority to mandate work hours, break times, dress codes, confidentiality, and team structures. We voluntarily grant this authority in exchange for a fair wage, and we trust the employer's ability to know and deliver on strategic objectives.

But government often acts like our employer, introducing intrusive controls despite the fact that we haven't agreed to them. And unlike a business owner, whose success depends on operating efficiently toward clear goals, the government has no such restrictions. The strategic objectives may be flawed, the plan of execution may be flawed and, most poignantly, the politicians may be flawed.

Politicians Are Not Kings

As more Americans see the failings of our elected officials and bureaucrats, we can no longer believe (if we ever did) that government functionaries understand our issues—or can magically make better choices—for our lives than we do and can.

Those who work in government are at least as flawed as the rest of us. Consider these recent stories of government employees misbehaving:

- The EPA employee who surfed porn all day on the taxpayers' dime
- IRS employees who audited their political enemies
- The Justice Department that spied on reporters
- GAO employees overspending on lavish conferences
- Secret Service agents on overseas assignments with prostitutes in their rooms
- The VA employee caught selling medications to patients

Countless headlines remind us of how *human* government employees are. So why do so many Americans approve of these people bossing the rest of us around?

The majority of local, state and federal employees are fine, law-abiding people, just like any cross-section of America. But to make any further leap—that they are better than those of us not in government at making decisions in our lives—is wishful thinking. Yet these are the people we entrust to fix the important problems in our lives.

Aren't some problems so important that we don't dare abandon them to government?

Are They Our "Betters?"

Cam Edwards hosts NRA News' *Cam and Company*, where he discusses not only Second Amendment news, but also freedom in general. He describes this approach as "The betters versus the bumpkins," referring to those in government who think they know better than we do how to live our lives. "Betters" see themselves as more sage, educated, and sophisticated than the rest of us, the "bumpkins" who can't be trusted to make complicated decisions on our own.

Both Democrats and Republicans encourage their "betters" to legislate decisions for the rest of us:

- Municipalities requiring reusable grocery bags or forcing non-compliant shoppers to pay a bag tax
- Local governments banning e-cigarettes in various locations, even shops that sell e-cigarettes
- School districts sending letters to parents whose children are deemed too fat
- States trying to pass laws that require counseling before a divorce can be filed
- States prohibiting the sale of alcohol on Sundays
- Local governments proposing "sin taxes" on products they feel are harmful

Aren't these decisions that individuals could—should—make for themselves?

There is no American who by birthright has the moral authority to control the rest of us.

Government officials who impose these bureaucratic whims are no better than those they are governing; they merely happen to hold a certain job. They are not endowed with some special birthright giving them the power to lord over us. We are, famously, all created equal.

Trust Is Reciprocal

Would you trust a neighbor who didn't trust you? Would you let that person choose your car or set your children's menu? Yet the government is that neighbor who does not trust you to make the best choices for yourself and your family: not to eat enough vegetables or buy the right showerhead. These issues aren't the government's business, yet it doesn't trust you to choose properly. Instead, it enacts laws mandating what you must do, and takes away your freedom to choose the best solution for yourself.

And even though public trust in government remains near historic lows, government controls more and more of the decisions in our lives. All because they deem you and me untrustworthy to make our own decisions. Why do we allow this to happen? Why did we cede control to a government that won't trust us?

Now imagine granting trust to your friends and neighbors, to individuals exercising their own freedoms, as they grant you reciprocal trust. Their choices would not be the same as yours. It might be uncomfortable to see such expressions of individual freedom: an untidy bustle of non-conformity and personal choice.

But consider the alternative.

CHAPTER 3

Central Control
or Personal Choice

Either you choose your actions or someone else chooses for you. In issues big or small, personal or professional, public or private, the dichotomy is the same.

You pick a restaurant or eat what the mess hall serves you. Choose your doctor or accept the VA services. Worship in your own way or...

For most people, what you eat and how you believe belong in the domain of personal choice. But what of all the other issues?

Social Issues: Control vs. Choice

Some social issues have a high level of agreement: No one lobbies to allow more child abuse or human trafficking. Condemnation of these ills is universal.

Other social issues don't have such unanimity. Despite massive spending and lobbying from all sides, the Fireworks issues (abortion, guns, schools, same-sex marriage) remain contentious. No side has convinced the other of its "rightness."

Perhaps this is because there are more fundamental principles preventing agreement. Perhaps when we examine these as issues of control versus choice, we may find common ground.

They're Both Wrong

Consider the Democrats and Republicans as broad representatives of an American divide on key social issues. Of course there are other parties, and factions within each party, but as a general shorthand these two have staked opposite positions, and will serve as each position's philosophical defenders.

And they're both wrong.

On issues that we, individually, can fix—on these Fireworks issues—both Republicans and Democrats imagine that central control and more bureaucracy is the answer. They think that we the people are incapable of self-control, of making wise choices, of living freely.

This condescension is uncivil. We are equal to the government officials, and it's our responsibility to prove that we can create private and voluntary answers to issues where the government "solution" usually makes a big problem worse.

Choice-based private answers exist. And they are less intrusive, less expensive, and less demeaning than the coercive public ones. When the right answer is private choice, more citizens need to step up and more politicians need to back off.

The Political Spectrum

Americans typically frame politics as a stark contrast:

- Liberal or Conservative
- Democrat or Republican
- Left or Right

But not everyone slots neatly into a category. Among elected officials, many neither conform to their party's actual platform nor always vote along party lines. And beyond individual variance, sizeable subgroups reflect the natural fracturing that arises from people who hold fundamental differences of opinion. There is a philosophical home, for example, for Blue Dog Democrats, Tea Party conservatives, pro-choice Republicans, and pro-gun Democrats.

Each party's platform fails to represent all of its members. And no political party at all claims to represent those who aren't political, or who find that neither party reflects their views. Is there a clearer, more consistent way of thinking, beyond this traditional left-right continuum?

Two Camps, Both Gray

Instead of evaluating political policy questions according to party-based dogma, consider these conflicting sentiments:

- It is better for individuals to make choices for themselves.
- It is better for governments to control people's choices.

Aside from some shades of gray, public-policy solutions favor one of these premises—and too often it's the second.

Picture a spectrum ranging from government control on one end to individual choice on the other. If the Republican Party platform on the Fireworks issues were plotted on this scale, it might look like this:

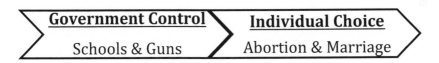

The Democratic Party platform suggests the opposite:

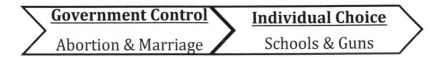

Overlapping Views

But consider a broader view that reveals areas where both parties agree. The shaded boxes below show agreement on issues of both individual choice and government control.

	DEMOCRATIC PARTY PLATFORM	
	Favor Individual Choice	*Favor Government Control*
Favor Individual Choice	• Groceries • Career • Religion • Lemonade Stand	• Guns • Schools • Minimum Wage
Favor Government Control	• Abortion • Marriage • Marijuana	• Courts • Police • Military • Stoplights

(Row group labeled: REPUBLICAN PARTY PLATFORM)

Although the Democratic Party platform favors individual choice on abortion, it favors government control on guns. And although the Republican Party platform favors individual choice on schools, it favors government control on same-sex marriage.

Casting issues as choice versus control provides an alternative to the traditional left-right language, and instead leaves a single question.

Who makes the decision, the government or the individual?

The shift gives us a different but consistent angle from which to suggest public policy, even when that policy contrasts with someone's personal position.

A person can:

- loathe guns and choose to never own one ...
- choose a traditional public school for his or her own children ...
- think that abortion is immoral ...
- believe that same-sex marriage isn't in keeping with his religious views ...

... but still believe that the government shouldn't control that decision for any individual.

A common thread is emerging, one at odds with political party orthodoxy and nightly news headlines. Recent polls confirm what I've been seeing for years, as I talk with voters of all political leanings: Americans more and more feel that it's not right to push their political views on others, nor is it any of the government's business to use its force for the same reason.

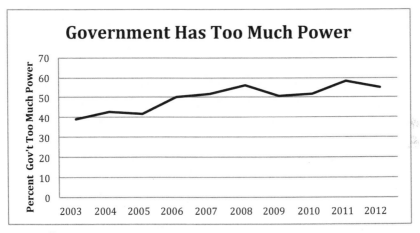

Source: Gallup, 2012

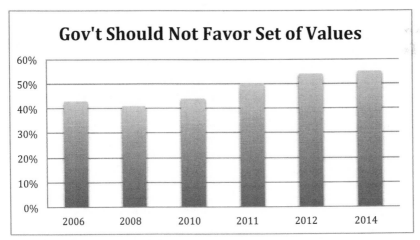

Source: CNN Poll, 2015

The platforms of the major political parties don't reflect these attitudes: each wants more government power enforcing their sets of values. But only theirs.

Beliefs at Conflict

Democrats are generally in favor of a larger and more federally regulated government. They believe that government knows what's best for individuals, and that benevolent government programs and virtuous government officials are most able to make the choices that make a better community. Republicans are generally in favor of a smaller, more locally controlled government. They believe that individuals, rather than a centrally planned government, know best how to make their own choices.

But these beliefs often conflict with practice. Many Republicans vote for their own pet form of larger government, while many Democrats promote unique local answers in their home districts.

If inconsistency between belief and practice plagues both parties, is this because each is internally inconsistent in its positions on issues of choice and control on social issues?

Democratic Party Platform: Top-Down, Except When...

The Democratic Party platform supports the idea that the government is best equipped to make most decisions for individuals. They support top-down policies for health care, education, energy, and the environment, among others. Democrats favor a national health insurance plan (Obamacare), nationally controlled education and its policies such as Common Core, the federal Environmental Protection Agency and its decisions that cover the entire country, and the Department of Energy's policies controlling nationwide energy production.

They believe that these sorts of policies and federal agencies provide the safety net and national standards that protect the most vulnerable among us.

In their platform, the Democrats say:

Schools:
The Democratic Party understands the importance of turning around struggling public schools. We will continue to strengthen all our schools and work to expand public school options for low-income youth, including magnet schools, charter schools, teacher-led schools, and career academies.

Guns:
We can focus on effective enforcement of existing laws, especially strengthening our background check system, and we can work together to enact common sense improvements—like reinstating the assault weapons ban and closing the gun show loophole—so that guns do not fall into the hands of those irresponsible, law-breaking few.

In other words, the Democrats, via the federal government, are there to make these decisions for you and your well-being.

But they don't want the government controlling abortion and marriage. Instead, Democrats want to leave those decisions to individuals.

Same-Sex Marriage:
We support marriage equality and support the movement to secure equal treatment under law for same-sex couples.

Abortion:
The President and the Democratic Party believe that women have a right to control their reproductive choices.

A question for Democrats:

Are people capable of making all of the decisions in their lives, or only some of the decisions in their lives?

Who Controls Her Body?

Either the government ought to control these decisions or the choice should be left to the individual. According to the Democratic Party platform, Democrats don't want the government included in abortion and marriage choices. Why, then, should government be involved in *any* individual choice, whether it be schools or gun ownership?

Recent implications of Obamacare highlight this inconsistency. Regarding abortion, Democrats say they don't want the government getting between a woman and her doctor. Yet Obamacare, with its numerous mandates and centralized control, has the government doing precisely that. When faced with this disparity, Democrats have a difficult time saying why one is right and the other not.

How should Democrats reconcile their principle that a woman has the right to choose an abortion, with their insistence that government must control her mammogram schedule? Does she control her body or does she not?

Perhaps It's All Just Too Complicated for Her

Do Democrats trust women to make their own decisions on abortion and couples to make their own decisions on marriage because these are the easy decisions?

Do they believe that choices about health insurance, schools, and self-defense are more difficult and thus can't be made by ordinary citizens without government guidance? It's as if Democrats are saying that we need a smart, centrally planned government, staffed with professional bureaucrats, to make these decisions for us. They imply that we need government wisdom to compensate for our shortsightedness and destructive impulses. It's as if they're patting a working mom's hand, telling the poor dear that guns and insurance and schools are just too complicated for her.

Democrats also imply that the bad decisions individuals might make if left to choose their own schools and guns will lead to worse schools and more gun violence. See Chapters 8 and 9 for evidence that refutes this view.

Republican Party Platform: Bottom-Up, Except When ...

The Republican Party platform supports individual choice and local control. And when government must be involved, Republicans prefer it be at the most local level—school boards and city councils, for example. Republicans with libertarian leanings have an even more "live and let live" attitude, believing that as long as their neighbors' decisions don't impact them, it's none of anyone's business.

Republicans favor school choice, seeing competition as a driving force to improve education. They promote public charter schools, private schools, and homeschooling as alternatives to the historical public school monopoly on the delivery of education. They recognize that as with any healthy marketplace, underperforming schools—schools that do not provide what their communities need—must innovate or fail, and that additional money alone is almost never the solution.

Republicans support the right of law-abiding Americans to choose their own form of self-defense, and largely support private firearms ownership with minimal restrictions.

But Republicans also make government bigger. Federal entitlement spending over the past 50 years has grown significantly more under Republican presidents than under Democratic presidents. The pledge in their platform to "return government to its proper role" rings hollow.

In their platform, the Republicans say:

Schools:
We applaud efforts to promote school choice initiatives that give parents more control over their children's education. By the same token, we defend the option for home schooling and call for vigilant enforcement of laws designed to protect family rights and privacy in education.

Guns:
We uphold the right of individuals to keep and bear arms, a right which antedated the Constitution and was solemnly confirmed by the Second Amendment. We acknowledge, support, and defend the law-abiding citizen's God-given right of self-defense.

It's a Matter of Faith

Republicans trust citizens to choose a school and to own a gun; however, they want the government to control decisions regarding abortion and same-sex marriage. Many Republicans are thus willing to apply the force of government to enshrine their biblical beliefs in law.

The Republican Party platform says as much:

Same-sex Marriage:
We recognize and honor the courageous efforts of those who bear the many burdens of parenting alone, even as we believe that marriage, the union of one man and one woman, must be upheld as the national standard, a goal to stand for, encourage, and promote through laws governing marriage.

Abortion:
We assert the sanctity of human life and affirm that the unborn child has a fundamental individual right to life, which cannot be infringed.

Barely Half Agree

And yet these platform planks are not supported by the whole body of Republicans. A full 48% of self-described Republicans do not want *Roe v. Wade* overturned, and 40% of self-described Republicans—just before the Supreme Court ruling assuring the right to same-sex marriage—thought same-sex marriage should be legal.

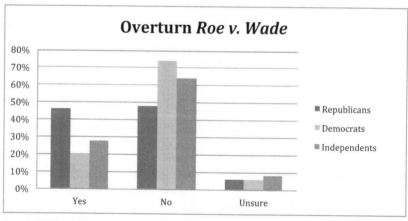

Source: CBS News Poll, 2013

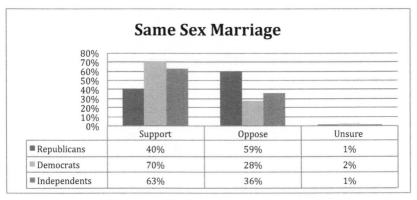

Same Sex Marriage

	Support	Oppose	Unsure
■ Republicans	40%	59%	1%
■ Democrats	70%	28%	2%
■ Independents	63%	36%	1%

Source: CNN Poll, 2015

A question for Republicans:

Are people capable of making all of the decisions in their lives, or only some of the decisions in their lives?

Either the government should control these decisions or individuals should. If the Republican platform trusts individuals on school choice and gun rights, why doesn't it trust individuals regarding abortion and same-sex marriage?

The key question is this: Does government control of abortion and marriage lead to fewer abortions and better quality marriages? See Chapters 7 and 10 for evidence that it does not.

Parties at a Crossroads

The Democratic and Republican parties need to decide who should choose: the individual or the state. And if the answer is individuals, then why should they be allowed to make only some decisions?

Regardless of how those questions are answered, problems remain. The Fireworks issues remain. And increasingly, the rank-and-file members of each party don't agree with their party bosses. Somebody needs to be able to solve these problems.

But if not the government, then who?

CHAPTER 4

WE CAN SOLVE OUR
OWN PROBLEMS

D o government officials really think we need to be coddled and micromanaged? When they dictate which bathroom faucet we can buy, how big our soda can be, or what health care is best for our family, they reveal a lack of trust in our ability to choose what's best for us. Officious bureaucrats imagine that like dependent children, we need endless laws and regulations—of their personal design—for our own good.

Whether from the left or the right the nannying continues, even while discontent with both Democrats and Republicans is on the rise. A 2014 Rasmussen poll showed 53% (up 6% from the previous year) saying that neither political party represents them.

Rise of the Independents

Voters are bristling at the constraints.

Whether it's against Republican Party control of abortion and marriage, or Democratic Party control of guns and schools, voters are rebelling against their own parties' platforms. Rank-and-file political stalwarts are becoming less conformist and more individualist, as voters on both sides come to resent a government that has grown too big and too powerful.

Yet both major parties continue to push policies supporting more government decisions and fewer individual choices. Voters are awakening to the disconnect between what they want and what the parties are providing, and this increasing disaffection shows up in the changing voter registration tallies.

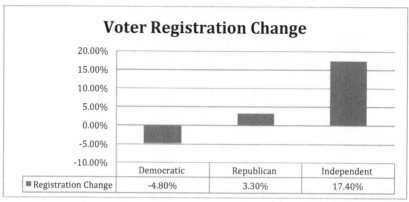

Voter Registration Change	Democratic	Republican	Independent
■ Registration Change	-4.80%	3.30%	17.40%

Source: ThirdWay.org, 2014

A recent study by ThirdWay.org, a "radical middle" organization that rejects the polarizing ideology of the major political parties, shows that in the past six years, voter registration has shifted noticeably. In their study of the ten states with the most competitive U.S. Senate races in 2014, independent voter registrations grew by more than 17%.

According to a Pew poll in 2014, 39% of voters nationally now consider themselves politically independent. This movement away from the two largest political parties comes at a time when approval ratings near historic lows for politicians on both sides of the aisle.

Americans say that political parties don't represent them.

In this context, "independent" includes not only registered members of the Independent Party, but also unaffiliated and "decline-to-state" voters, all of whose burgeoning registrations reflect an increasing support for gun rights, school choice, legal abortion, and same-sex marriage.

America's Independent Streak

From the two-year-old telling his mommy that he can do it himself, to a student rebelling against a lesson plan that holds no interest for her, to an employee wanting autonomy at work, to homeowners preferring to choose their own household products, Americans don't want to be bossed around. They want to be in control, not coddled.

Ask a child what he wants to be when he grows up. I have yet to hear anyone say he wants to sit on the couch and wait for his next welfare check. Americans have ambition, ideas, and independence. They want to *earn* the best life they can make for themselves and their children.

Although the neediest Americans rightfully rely on some government assistance, most Americans don't strive to be supported by anyone. They aspire to more than the minimal government-paid-for apartment or phone or clothing or cheese. In the same way that college graduates do not want to be dependent on their parents, neither do most Americans want to depend on the government—not for basic goods, and not to be told what *is* good.

We want to provide for ourselves, and to solve most problems ourselves.

Even difficult and personal ones.

My Answers Need Not Be Yours

Many women describe themselves as pro-life when it comes to *their* own situation, *their* own choice and *their* own decision. If they had an unplanned pregnancy, they would not choose an abortion *for themselves.* Yet they might not want the government limiting choices for others, given each woman's difficult and unique circumstances. For a personal-pro-life woman, her choice to not have an abortion starts and ends with her, and she prefers to extend that autonomy for such a personal decision to all women.

Likewise for same-sex marriage. Many people who don't believe same-sex marriage is right or moral also don't want the government controlling that decision for others. According to a 2013 Gallup poll, more than 75% of Americans know someone who is gay, and more than half have had someone personally tell them that they are gay or lesbian. People who in the past may not have accepted the openly gay now find their attitudes changing as the issue comes closer to home.

Education choices are equally as personal. Many supporters of traditional neighborhood public schools have no interest in limiting choices for other families. Children in supporters' families might attend a great public school in a great school district, where parents know the teachers and principals personally. Supporters' neighborhood schools might have high graduation and college acceptance rates, but families of attendees there also likely know that not all public schools perform that well. Many have seen *Waiting For Superman*, the award-winning documentary about failing schools, or seen dismal school success rates and know that there has to be a better way for *all* kids. Choosing the traditional public school option is not, for these families, reason to restrict that choice for others.

Many people don't like guns and would never choose to own one, but they nonetheless wouldn't want the government deciding for others how they should choose to defend themselves and their family. As of 2014, a majority of Americans say it's more important to protect the right to own guns than it is to further gun control. The self-reliant attitude is, "I make my choice. You make yours." Acknowledging how long law enforcement might take to arrive at a home incident, and recognizing the responsibility of a family to ensure its own safety, even those who don't own guns are now more likely to support others' choices to do so.

Americans want independence from condescending, controlling busybodies—especially for issues of such profoundly personal consequence. And they know that to be granted that independence means not imposing their personal choices on everyone else.

So what happens to politicians who act otherwise?

Social Issues Warriors Lose

As Americans think about political issues more in terms of choice versus control, and trust less in the government's ability to fix anything, they become increasingly irritated with the single-minded focus—from both parties—on social issues. And candidates, Republican or Democrat, who stake their political fortunes solely on social issues learn at the ballot box how out of touch they are.

Republicans Lose

In the presidential election of 2012, Sandra Fluke, a woman smart enough to attend Georgetown law school, testified to Congress that if the insurance policy provided by her Jesuit university didn't pay for her birth control, she was powerless to obtain it. Fluke said that the government should force the University to offer that type of coverage. She claimed that over the course of a three-year law school degree, her own birth control would cost $3,000, yet a Target store near the Georgetown campus offered birth control pills for $9 per month, or $324 for that three-year span. Her exaggerated hardship claim exposed this as a purely political issue.

Nonetheless, Democrats capitalized on the idea of a religious organization denying women access to reproductive choices, and played the "war on women" narrative to their advantage, portraying Republicans as knuckle-dragging Neanderthals who wanted women back in the kitchen—barefoot and pregnant.

Republicans reinforced that narrative, giving Democrats ample "war on women" gaffes in that election year. U.S. Senate candidates Todd Akin and Richard Mourdock both made social issues a focus of their campaigns, to disastrous results.

Todd Akin

Todd Akin entered elective politics in 1988, and progressed from a Missouri State Legislative career to United States Congress in 2001. In 2012, while polling ahead of his Democrat rival Claire McCaskill in Missouri's U.S. Senate race, he said, during an interview about exceptions for abortion due to rape, that it's rare for women to get pregnant during a "legitimate rape." He elaborated that the female body has a way to try to shut down pregnancy.

A predictable uproar ensued on both sides of the aisle. Candidates, elected officials, party bosses and third-party funders such as American Crossroads and the National Republican Senatorial Committee, denounced Akin's comments, calling on him to resign. Republicans nationwide, many of whom were in their own close election battles, fielded questions about exceptions to abortion, and whether they agreed with Akin's statements. His comments became the focus not only of his campaign, but the campaigns of *every other Republican nationwide.*

Akin soon apologized, saying that he misspoke, and meant "forcible rape"—which didn't diminish the uproar. Isn't rape by definition forcible, or was Akin indicating that some rapes might be consensual? His comments, and the Republicans who stood by him, gave more than enough evidence that the Democrats' "war on women" campaign was not just rhetoric.

> *Akin, a social-issues warrior, lost 55%–39%.*

In 2014 Akin published *Firing Back: Taking on the Party Bosses and Media Elite to Protect Our Faith and Freedom*, in which he regretted apologizing, and reiterated his belief that it's rare for women to get pregnant during a rape. He is a jackass and grade-A idiot.

Richard Mourdock

Richard Mourdock was Indiana's State Treasurer, and won the U.S. Senate primary against Richard Lugar in 2012. Two months after Akin's firestorm, and a mere two weeks before the general election, Mourdock answered a question on abortion:

> I believe that life begins at conception. The only exception I have to have an abortion is in that case of the life of the mother. I just struggled with it myself for a long time but I came to realize: Life is that gift from God that I think even if life begins in that horrible situation of rape, that it is something that God intended to happen.

Again, the response came quickly from both parties. He was accused of saying that God intends for rape to happen. Mourdock apologized, and tried to restate his comment in a different way, but the damage was done.

> *This social-issues warrior lost 50%–44%.*

The result was not only that both of these Republicans lost their elections, but also that the Democrats effectively used Akin and Mourdock as examples of what the entire Republican Party must believe. Every Republican candidate and office holder during the 2012 election cycle was tarred with that broad brush, even though nearly every one of them condemned the comments. The tarnish even spread to Republican Presidential candidate, Mitt Romney. Despite his denouncement of both statements, the stain-by-association endured.

Although the Akin and Mourdock comments were not an accurate representation of the overall Republican Party membership, the

Democrats' "war on women" narrative succeeded, giving them significant electoral victories. Battleground states skewed overwhelmingly for Barack Obama, and Republicans lost eight Congressional seats.

Democrats Lose

The Democrats won big in 2010 and 2012 leveraging the "war on women" narrative. Why should 2014 have been any different?

Mark Udall

In the 2014 election for U.S. Senate from Colorado, Democrat incumbent Senator Mark Udall carried this "war on women" theme so far that he was dubbed "Mark Uterus" during the campaign, as roughly half his ads referenced abortion and contraception. NARAL Pro-Choice Colorado, a group supporting Udall, even ran an ad in the final weeks of the campaign implying that if Republican challenger Cory Gardner won, there would be a condom shortage.

Meanwhile, Gardner was on record in favor of making birth control pills available over-the-counter, without a doctor's prescription. The idea of him being in favor of banning birth control seemed far-fetched to voters.

Why didn't this approach work for Senator Udall in 2014, when it played so successfully nationwide in 2010 and 2012?

First, there were no Todd Akins or Richard Mourdocks making national news with their asinine statements.

Second, with Obamacare's birth-control mandate in place, voters no longer believed that access to birth control was a disputed issue. Since access was settled in law, voters saw Udall's tactics as a cynical political ploy.

Finally, since 2014 was the third consecutive election cycle trumpeting the "war on women," the the single issue balloon had lost its air. Women were annoyed and insulted at Udall's implication that women were so shallow that they cared about nothing except birth control and abortion.

This narrative outlived its usefulness, and lost credibility over multiple election cycles when voters, especially women, stopped believing that any politician was going to take away their access to legal birth control or abortion.

With his exclusive focus on social issues, Udall's result mirrored Akin's and Mourdock's when he lost to Cory Gardner.

This social-issues warrior lost 48.5%–46%.

Akin and Mourdock and Udall lost because they intruded too far into issues that were both intimately personal and not the proper domain of government. In a September 2014 Gallup poll that asked "What do you think is the most important problem facing the country today?" abortion and same-sex marriage polled at only 1% each, not even in the top 10.

Voters see these private issues as none of the government's business. Politicians who disagree lose.

Michael Bloomberg

Michael Bloomberg earned his billions (current net worth: $37B) in the private sector before being elected Mayor of New York City in 2001. Throughout his twelve-year tenure in that office, he advocated all manner of government intrusions into citizens' lives. Among his proposed bans:

- Smoking in commercial establishments
- Smoking in public places
- Cigarette sales to those under 21
- Sales of flavored tobacco products
- Smoking e-cigarettes in public places
- Cigarette in-store displays
- Cars in Times Square
- Cars from driving in newly created bike lanes
- Cars causing congestion below 60th Street in Manhattan
- Speeding in residential "slow zones"
- Illegal guns—as Bloomberg defined them
- Sodium levels in processed foods
- Trans-fats in restaurants
- Loud headphones
- Styrofoam packaging in single-service food items
- Sodas larger than 16 ounces

- Collection of yard waste and grass clippings during certain times of the year
- Organic food waste from landfills
- Commercial music louder than 45 decibels
- Chain restaurant menus without calorie counts
- The posting of signs in "city-owned grassy areas"
- Non-fuel-efficient cabs
- New taxicabs that weren't Nissan NV200s
- Greenhouse gas emissions
- Government buildings that weren't LEED-certified
- Non-hurricane-proof buildings in coastal areas
- Black roofs
- Construction cranes more than 25 years old
- No. 6 and No. 4 "heavy" heating oils
- Less than a 2:1 ratio of female and male restrooms in new public buildings
- Cell phones in schools
- Two-term limits for city elected officials

This list is exhausting; that's the point. Bloomberg's conceit of knowing what was "for our own good" seemed limitless. He lamented the health ills of tobacco, salt, trans-fats, and large sodas, which gave him reason to treat the adults in his city like children as he tried to restrict those legal products. His tactic: invent a problem regarding the actions of free adults, then mandate a government "fix."

Some of Bloomberg's proposals passed. Some, like the ban on large sodas, were rejected by the First Department of the State Supreme Court's Appellate Division as unconstitutional.

Bloomberg epitomizes Cam Edwards' idea of "The Betters versus The Bumpkins." Bloomberg truly believes he knows better than those who are less educated or wealthy. He once said:

> I've got the greatest job in the world. There's no other job in government where cause and effect is so tightly coupled where you can make a difference every day in so many different ways and in so many different people's lives. It's a great challenge.

Never mind whether we want or need him to "make a difference" in our lives.

Although Bloomberg could propose these measures only in New York City, where his compliant residents re-elected him twice, his reputation as someone who was butting in to citizens' lives spread nationwide.

In 2006 he started an organization called "Mayors Against Illegal Guns" (MAIG). MAIG's original stated goal was to "support efforts to educate policy makers, as well as the press and the public, about the consequences of gun violence and promote efforts to keep guns out of the hands of criminals"—laudable on its surface. Who wouldn't want to disarm lawbreakers?

But that's not what MAIG really wanted.

Although at peak more than 1000 mayors supported MAIG, they began distancing themselves when it became clear that MAIG's answer was to ban guns for all citizens, not just criminals. Many mayors, with a goal of trying to reduce crime, recognized that keeping guns in the hands of law-abiding citizens aided their cause.

Eleven of the member mayors also found themselves in trouble with the law, facing charges from bribery to DUI to downloading child pornography. Their hypocrisy sparked a parody name: "*Illegal* Mayors Against Guns." Amid the mayors' legal problems and the significant reduction in membership, MAIG slowly receded from prominence.

But Bloomberg was not done. On the day after the 2012 Sandy Hook shootings, a new organization, "Moms Demand Action For Gun Sense In America" (Moms Demand), launched and joined forces with MAIG. Moms Demand "was created to demand action from legislators, state and federal; companies; and educational institutions to establish common-sense gun reforms." Unlike MAIG, which leveraged mayors around the country, Moms Demand positioned gun control as a women's issue.

Through these organizations and their associated political action committees, Bloomberg worked to influence gun control laws at the state level. Massive donations went to gun-control candidates and organizations, and to sponsor gun control bills. Bloomberg and MAIG hired lobbyists in key states to help write and enact local gun control legislation.

But money alone couldn't save candidates focused only on gun control. Bloomberg contributed $350,000 to two Colorado State Senators,

John Morse and Angela Giron, trying to prevent their recall for their controversial gun control votes. Senator Morse, the Colorado State Senate President in 2013, set the agenda and tone for all of the gun control bills proposed that year—bills so extreme that they incited recalls for the two senators.

I supported the recall, and actively produced numerous radio and TV ads urging Morse's removal. Bloomberg outspent our pro-recall forces by six to one.

He also spent $150,000 to try to unseat Sheriff David Clarke from Milwaukee County, Wisconsin, who suggested that citizens arm themselves to help defend against criminals. Clarke said in a local TV ad:

> With officers laid-off and furloughed, simply calling 9-1-1 and waiting is no longer your best option. You can beg for mercy from a violent criminal, hide under the bed, or you can fight back; but are you prepared? Consider taking a certified safety course in handling a firearm so you can defend yourself until we get there. You have a duty to protect yourself and your family. We're partners now.

This prompted Bloomberg to say, "This one is personal to me." He contributed $150,000 to Clarke's pro-gun-control opponent, all in response to a local ad, by a local sheriff, for a local crime issue. Sheriff Clarke told *National Review*'s Charles C. W. Cooke:

> I didn't see this as a national question when I spoke out. The ad was meant in response to some local crime issues. I couldn't have dreamed of being catapulted into the national spotlight. When it started to grow, I tried to corral it and push it away. This is my hometown. I'm just trying to make a difference here.

Bloomberg's intrusion into local gun-control issues failed. Both the Colorado recalls and Sheriff Clarke's re-election were successful.

Bloomberg is continuing with a $50 million campaign against retailers who refuse to ban law-abiding gun owners from carrying a concealed firearm on the retailers' property. Though not a political campaign, this is another example of a political cause focused entirely on a social issue.

For his obsession with gun control and his ban-what-I-don't-like approach, Bloomberg has become the poster child for "government knows best" politicians. Americans who trust that we know our own lives best, and who believe that we solve our own problems better than any government official can, are standing up against this type of control.

Regardless of affiliation, voters are ousting politicians who focus too exclusively on social issues. At the ballot box, they are acknowledging that not only are certain topics more properly private matters—for which social-issues zealots will be voted out—but also that in almost every domain into which it intrudes, government ruins almost everything.

GOVERNMENT RUINS
NEARLY EVERYTHING

W hy does everything the government touches become worse? Perhaps not *everything*. Government is indispensable for national defense, police, courts—and maybe putting a human on the moon, although recent private efforts by commercial entities like SpaceX and Virgin Galactic might suggest a challenge to government primacy in the latter role.

Yet we continue to think that the government should be able to knit us together with regulations, legislate a Band-aid law to bridge moral divides, or mandate "solutions" to the personal, universal, profoundly human dilemmas that both divide and unite us, issues of faith and love and safety and family—none of which the government is equipped to address. Not because public employees aren't big-hearted or wise enough, but because the incentives are all wrong.

The government as an institution has incentives to let problems stay and grow, while the private sector does not. Individuals in the private sector prosper by solving problems, not by perpetuating the cultures that maintain then.

Combine government's ineptness with the fact that it's the only entity we authorize to use force on our behalf. Who wouldn't wonder at the wisdom of that recipe?

A Matter of Incentives

The private sector is that part of the economy run by individuals and companies, not under state control, usually operated for a profit. It's the "free" part of "free market," where "free" doesn't means without cost, but voluntary. Quite unlike government interactions, transactions in a free market happen only when both sides agree that they prefer what's on the opposite side of any exchange to what's on their own side. Nothing in a free market happens without this mutual consent, and when any transaction happens, it benefits both sides.

The Private Sector Works

The private sector works because every transaction creates value, since both parties gain something more valuable than they had before. Which means that every business has the same target: please consumers enough that they will voluntarily exchange their money for the business's products or services.

With the profit motive as incentive, businesses invest in research and development, risk resources on new products, and establish new markets. Misjudging the market has consequences: consumers will choose alternatives—and there are always alternatives. Unlike government entities undiminished (and unpunished) by failure after failure, private sector enterprises that misjudge or mismanage enough will fail. It's that failure, Schumpeter's "creative destruction," that allows innovation, by freeing resources that aren't being best used. When was the last time government resources were reallocated to something more useful?

Consider Colgate Kitchen Entrees. In 1982, Colgate, the toothpaste company, sought to capture the ready-to-eat meal market. Busy consumers wanted fast and healthy alternatives in the frozen-food aisle.

But they didn't want them from Colgate, whose Kitchen Entrees failed even before launch. Customers equated Colgate with clean teeth, and they associated eating with the opposite. Colgate's brand was so strong that customers couldn't square it with tasty food—or food of any kind. But Colgate alone took the risk and they alone suffered the financial consequences of failure. *No taxpayers were on the hook.*

In 1996 McDonald's failed even more spectacularly. Attempting to lure more adults, it created the Arch Deluxe, billed as "the burger with the grown-up taste." Ads featured McDonald's signature Ronald McDonald mascot doing adult things like wearing a business suit and playing golf. The company was trying to appeal to the parents who bought Happy Meals for their kids, but nothing for themselves.

After spending a staggering $100 million to market the new burger,

McDonald's pulled the product in what is recognized as one of the most expensive ad flops in history. Yet only McDonald's took the risk, and only they suffered the financial consequences. *No taxpayers were on the hook.*

Both Colgate and McDonald's had the freedom to dream up these ideas around their boardroom tables. They alone designed the products and marketing campaigns. They alone invested. They alone assessed the sales and tallied the failures. And they alone absorbed the losses. Both Colgate and McDonald's survived their bad product decisions. Other companies were not so lucky.

Kodak was *the* name in film for more than one hundred years, its brand as iconic as its ubiquitous yellow film boxes. They sold cameras as well, boosting ongoing film sales. Even film processing counters used Kodak processing. The film market, top to bottom, was Kodak's.

Although Kodak was among the first to develop digital technology, its worry about cannibalizing its film business prevented the aggressive market shift that the new technologies demanded. Competitors rushed in, and Kodak was left in the dust. In 2012 Kodak's bankruptcy filing signaled its sad end, but because Kodak's own business decisions caused its bankruptcy, *no taxpayers were on the hook.*

Companies in the private sector can make such mistakes and even ruin their business, leaving only ripple impacts on the public. Or they can please consumers and succeed.

In 1994, Jeff Bezos started Amazon.com in his garage, with money he borrowed from his parents. Within the first month, Amazon.com was posting sales of $20,000 per week. The next year, Bezos raised $8 million in private venture capital.

Remember how we viewed internet-based shopping in 1994. Buying a book online sounded baffling and futuristic. How would you browse the bookshelf or thumb through a particular book? Would your payment be secure? Would shipping costs be prohibitive? The questions were new and the concepts strange. But Jeff Bezos had the vision and took the risks. He didn't ask (or force) taxpayers to invest in what at the time sounded a little crazy.

Barely 20 years later, Amazon.com has passed Walmart to become the world's largest retailer, with a market cap of well over $200 billion. What started with books has become a marketplace for almost everything, one built on supplying exactly what consumers want. Had Bezos failed he might have lost the funds that he or his parents or his private investors risked. The rewards are (and the failures would have been) theirs alone.

Government Doesn't Work

Government fails in so many arenas largely because—unlike private exchanges—each transaction is not voluntary. People lose value most times that they interact with the government, whether it's submitting to a capricious bureaucracy or purchasing some non-competitive (but mandated) product, or obtaining a redundant license or complying with a burdensome regulation or any number of other compulsory and pica-yune annoyances. Citizens exchange their time or hard-earned money for something they neither want nor need. They lose value.

Additionally, government isn't constrained by market forces; its main source of revenue is taxation. So you and I, because we produce something of actual value, get the privilege of shipping part of our wages to them. And then we cross our fingers and hope they don't waste our money on ridiculous things.

But they *do* waste our money on ridiculous things. Why? Because the incentives are backwards: safety regardless of cost, a vague "common good" over individual prosperity, notions of social engineering that don't comport with most people's sensibilities. Most especially, no penalty for failure or risky decisions, not for the institutions or for the bureaucrats behind them.

Beyond that, each year, every government agency spends every dime allocated to it—regardless of need—because they want to make sure that next year's appropriations are even higher. Ronald Reagan's observance from 50+ years ago is still true today:

> No government ever voluntarily reduces itself in size. Government programs, once launched, never disappear. Actually, a government bu-reau is the nearest thing to eternal life we'll ever see on this earth!

Price No Object

Imagine a fictional private company, Acme T-Shirts, created to capitalize on a market niche for casual wear with an important message. They need a new website, a quality one at a good price. To sell across the country they need to calculate sales taxes and shipping by state. They need to ship efficiently, protect customer data, and process payments.

Acme has a tight budget, because every dollar spent on the website is money unavailable for employee salaries or owner compensation. When choosing a website provider, Acme will weigh cost against projected performance. In no case will it choose the most expensive vendor solely because it's the most expensive.

The government doesn't work like Acme. Certainly not when building HealthCare.gov, the website created by the Department of Health and Human Services (HHS) to comply with the Patient Protection and Affordable Care Act. Of course a website that allows people to enroll in health insurance is much more complicated than one selling T-shirts, but does the government follow the same process in selecting a web designer as any private company must? No. Since HHS employees suffered no consequences for overspending, price did not matter when HHS shopped for vendors. While Acme's owners want to spend as efficiently as possible to create optimal profit margins, HHS employees get paid the same, regardless of website costs.

If Acme spent all of its revenue on its website, forgoing expenses for employees, raw materials, and office rent, it would go out of business. What happened when HHS spent too much on their website? Despite an original budget of $93 million, the lowest estimate for the site's actual cost is $834 million. HHS spent more than *eight times* the original budget. No one got fired. No government employees had their pay cut. HHS didn't go out of business. *The taxpayers were on the hook.*

The government has no reason to be effective when the risks are offloaded to the taxpayers, *as they always are.* And rather than innovating, officials instead work to insulate themselves from blame. In a cover-your-ass atmosphere, bureaucrats follow policy, even when those procedures are outdated or misguided or partisan or Pollyannaish. Yet, unlike in private enterprise, those ineffective practices are not self-correcting. The marketplace, both of ideas and of commerce, cannot do its necessary role of winnowing nonperforming government institutions.

Still, some optimistic people like to think the government can solve great social problems.

It can't.

But We Keep Hoping

We continue to trust government with our biggest problems. Year after year, we hope that the government will solve the most important societal and cultural issues, but they never do. Nonetheless, we elect more of the same, regardless of political party, and (no surprise) we keep getting more of the same.

Why do we keep hoping?

Wrongs are inescapable and overwhelming: poverty and violence at home, war and beheadings overseas, cultural and technological upheavals—all of which feel too big for us to eradicate. Big-government advocates craft heartstring-tugging arguments that persuade us to believe that the next government fix will work. But it never does.

Decade after decade, government employees implement "solutions" that make the problem worse. Then they tell us that the fix for this is yet more government. Believing that story is akin to taking a medicine that only makes you sicker with each dose.

Consider the following speech, presented to the Economic Club of New York:

> In short, it is a paradoxical truth that tax rates are too high today and tax revenues are too low and the soundest way to raise the revenues in the long run is to cut the rates now. The experience of a number of European countries and Japan have borne this out. This country's own experience with tax reduction in 1954 has borne this out. And the reason is that only full employment can balance the budget, and tax reduction can pave the way to that employment. The purpose of cutting taxes now is not to incur a budget deficit, but to achieve the more prosperous, expanding economy which can bring a budget surplus.

Although this sounds like it could be from a Republican presidential candidate in the 2016 field, it is actually from December 1962. The speaker was President John F. Kennedy.

This sounds current because the problems of 50 years ago are still with us. And nothing the government has done or is going to do will fix them.

Can the Government Fix Failing Schools?

The U.S. Department of Education opened its doors in 1980. In their 35-year history, how have they helped or hurt education? According to the National Association of Education Progress, 66% of fourth graders are "below proficient" in reading, which means they are not reading at grade level.

At its inception the Department of Education's annual budget was $14 billion. For fiscal year 2016, the President is asking for more than $73 billion. In all, they have spent more than $1.5 trillion *of our money* in the past 35 years.

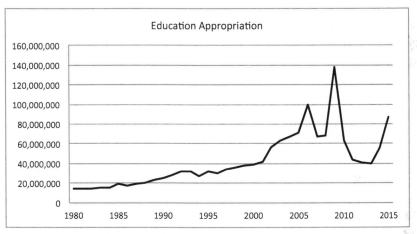

Source: U.S. Department of Education Budget History Tables

For all this spending, what does the Department of Education have to show for it? Ask two-thirds of American fourth graders—but don't do it in writing. Those kids can't read.

Our kids do no better in other subjects. According to the Paris-based Organization for Economic Cooperation and Development:

> Overall, according to the U.S. Department of Education, American students' rankings in math have slipped from 24th to 29th compared to the last test in 2010. In science, they've gone from 19th to 22nd, and from 10th to 20th in reading.

The U.S. continues to fall in education rankings compared to other countries despite decades of massive spending. Good intentions at the Department of Education aren't enough to improve schools, especially when their continuing prescription in the face of failure is to spend more each year.

We keep hoping that schools will get better, but excepting certain gains from charter schools and innovative private schools, schools in general are not improving.

Government can't fix failing schools.

Can the Government Fix Gun Violence?

Elected officials insist that more gun-control legislation will succeed in reducing gun violence. Yet at both the federal and state levels they pass laws whose only result is to do the opposite. Only when gun control laws are repealed does gun violence go down.

Even with proof that gun control doesn't reduce gun crime, the common governmental response to gun violence is to pass laws that make the problem worse.

Government can't fix gun violence.

Can the Government Reduce the Number of Abortions?

Let's ask first whether the government is even interested in reducing the number of abortions, considering that the government spends millions of dollars annually funding organizations that provide them. Easy access to birth control has decreased the need for abortions overall, but no documentation attests that the abortion rate is lower for those receiving free government-provided birth control compared to those who pay for their own.

One fact is certain: women choose abortion largely for financial reasons, including being unemployed or underemployed, not making enough to support a child, or being forced to live with an abuser in order to afford supporting a child. With taxes, fees, and regulations on the rise at every level, the government is not doing anything to ease the financial stress that might lead a woman to choose an abortion. A stronger economy would mean less financial stress on everyone, women included.

Government can't reduce the number of abortions.

Can the Government Fix Broken Marriages?

Instead of fixing broken marriages, the government provides incentives not to get married. Its perverse tax code subsidizes children outside of marriage. U.S. taxpayers fund more than $1 trillion in anti-poverty programs, many for single mothers who could lose their funding if they get married. Misguided compassion with government largesse translates into rewarding a single mother for having more children.

The tax code also penalizes married couples in certain circumstances. A couple with a large income disparity saves money filing jointly. But when their incomes are more equal, they are penalized with a larger tax bill—a blow for gender equality. Tax-code tinkering and social engineering fail to produce more stable marriages, and often work against that goal.

Government can't fix broken marriages.

Don't You Dare

Too many Americans, upon spotting a problem, reflexively suggest that, "The government needs to do something," or, "There ought to be a law." Maybe there ought not. Given the government's track record of making problems worse, why would we consider putting it in charge of fixing anything outside its Constitution-derived functions? If the Fireworks issues in this book—abortion, same-sex marriage, guns and schools—are that important, we need to say to each other, "Don't you dare let the government try to fix them!"

We the people, the citizens, need to take ownership of resolving these social issues ourselves. Meaningful advancements come more through private efforts and free-market solutions than from government fixes, and we need to examine why. What is it that private enterprise can do that government cannot, and how can we use those lessons to fix our own social issues?

Free Market: a Win-Win

Businesses succeed when they please customers—and there are always customers seeking their own unique mix of products and services. Which means endless opportunities for producers to succeed by catering to those desires. The possibility of profit, the universal matchmaker, is the compelling lure, and realizing those profits is the validation of the win-win nature of a free market.

A Store for You and a Store for Me

The free market improves the plight of everyone, even poor people, better than government ever could. According to Arthur Brooks of the American Enterprise Institute:

> Since 1970, the percentage of the world's population living on a dollar a day or less has decreased by 80 percent. Is this because of the fabulous success of the United Nations or U.S. foreign aid? Of course not. It is because of globalization, free trade, and entrepreneurship. In short, it is because of free enterprise, which is truly America's gift to the world's poor.

Store owners know that the free market is purely voluntary. They know that if you don't like a store you won't shop there, since there are always alternatives. So each owner must find a way to woo her customers: she can offer the cheapest or most up-to-date products, or offer the best customer service, or find some other way to meet her customers' needs. Customers do the reverse, choosing the stores best suited for them, and rewarding those stores with their business.

Store owners and customers both win with every purchase. Buyers might choose Walmart for the best price or Whole Foods for specialty items. No one forces Whole Foods to lower their prices, and no one forces Walmart to carry specialty items. As customers, we understand the differences between the stores—differences that the stores themselves actively cultivate with their own brand.

A store's brand tells consumers if it's the right fit—whether its customers are bargain hunters or trendsetters or wallflowers or divas. The free market creates stores for everyone, without some special government mandate on how many organic or cut-rate or high-end stores a community needs. Nor is some prescribed minimum quality the purview of government. In today's reputational marketplace, no business gets a free pass on poor service. Opinion sites like Yelp, Angie's List, and Urbanspoon let consumers communicate directly, democratizing the sanctioning process that in the past might have fallen to some government agency to enforce.

What the Government Couldn't Do

If the government isn't needed to ensure a thriving marketplace, does that mean it has no place in commerce? Perhaps it has a responsibility to foster innovation?

The 3D Printing Boom

Consider 3D Printing. Charles Hull filed the first patent for 3D printing in 1986, which at the time sounded like something out of *Star Trek*. Yet the idea was viable enough to support creating 3D Systems, a company Hull co-founded, and which today remains a marketplace leader. Their first industrial 3D printers sold in 1988 for more than $100,000.

That first patent signaled the start of competition and innovation, spurring other inventors to cycle through new methods and technologies. Yet for 20 years, while inching incrementally towards mass viability, 3D printing remained a niche and high-end industrial process. Until 2009, when after 23 years of private-sector development, commercially viable 3D printers became available for home consumers and mass industry adoption.

> *3D Printers are now available for well under $1000. From Walmart.*

At this price and ubiquity, applications are endless: from model airplanes to automobile prototypes, consumer products to aerospace components, even medicine. In 2012, doctors used a 3D printer to save the life of an infant who suffered a collapsed windpipe. Because everyone's airway is unique, no one-size-fits-all implant could work. Relying on a CT scan of Kaiba Gionfriddo's windpipe, doctors 3D-printed a custom splint for him, using a material that would change shape as he grew. Three weeks after surgery, he no longer needed a ventilator; today Kaiba is an active, healthy four-year-old.

Spurred by the free-market rewards that 3D printing has given to its pioneers, the technology is changing the world for the better, and its full impacts have yet to be felt.

Now imagine the federal government creating 3D printing instead. They would empanel a blue ribbon commission, appoint a 3D printing czar, pass protectionist legislation to shelter craft industries, spend "stimulus" tax money for research and development, hire expensive consultants to determine the most appropriate applications, fight over who should get subsidized 3D printers, and determine whether 3D printers should be considered sexist. That would be in the first year.

Then would follow the Congressional investigations about cost overruns and cronyism, protests over components being manufactured in non-union shops, and presidential pardons for those who skimmed money from the project. That might take a little longer.

After 30 years, 3D printers would still be a *Star Trek* fantasy.

The LASIK Choice

The cost of most medical care routinely outpaces inflation. Hiding prices behind the shroud of insurance complexity and cultural taboos will do that.

Yet in a marketplace where price is public, where practitioners compete for customers, even medical costs can come down—dramatically. Even as its entire field of treatment has been revolutionized, vision correction costs have declined while methods have improved, especially for LASIK (Laser-In-Situ Keratomileusis).

Because it's elective, corrective eye surgery is subject to market forces in ways that an emergency appendectomy is not. Consumers consider price when choosing a provider; doctors use price as one differentiator. When customers show—with their dollars—that demand for LASIK is high, more doctors enter the field, keeping prices in check. In addition, technical innovations that improve treatment reward their inventors, and widespread vision improvement boosts the industry's reputation as a whole.

The result is a virtuous cycle that runs counter to most insurance-covered procedures and to virtually all government services. Public pricing and private choice create efficiencies.

Evolving from the first laser vision correction on humans in 1988, the corneal surgery now known as LASIK has been the world's most common elective medical procedure for more than a decade. And still most health insurance does not cover the cost: "Not medically necessary," insurers say. With government intruding ever more into choosing what coverage is medically necessary, LASIK costs will remain unreimbursed.

That hasn't stopped consumers. More than 12 million Americans, and 30 million people worldwide, have undergone the procedure, even at $2,000 per eye. Why do they spend that much money just to see better—to avoid the inconvenience of glasses or contacts?

Because they can.

Because marketplace innovations and competition have made this life-changing procedure easy and affordable. Because choice, free-market forces, and the profit motive work.

The Airbnb Travel Transformation

Choice is also at the center of a transformation in the travel industry.

Airbnb was founded in 2007 by two 27-year-old San Franciscans struggling to pay their rent. During a busy conference, with all hotels at capacity, they had the idea to rent out air mattresses (thus *Airbnb*) on their living room floor for $80 each per night. Three people responded, one an international traveler. Each got a mattress. The travel industry got a revolution.

According to Airbnb:

> Airbnb hosts share their spaces in 190 countries and more than 34,000 cities. All you have to do is enter your destination and travel dates into the search bar to discover distinctive places to stay, anywhere in the world.

These distinctive places range from crash-pad futons to ultra-modern villas in Bali. Guests save between 20–50% from more traditional accommodations, while micropreneurial property owners capitalize on the opportunities of a new service economy. As private hosts with intimate knowledge of local sites, owners also help make travelers' stays more distinctive.

The glue keeping this peer-to-peer marketplace together? Trust.

Recognizing how essential common trust is to its marketplace, Airbnb has created systems to amplify it: guests and hosts may contact one another before booking, and feedback systems rate both hosts and guests. Guests can even connect their Facebook page to their application, leveraging their own *social proof* as a means to convince hosts of their trustworthiness, since hosts can choose which guests to allow. Both guests and hosts have incentive to appear—and be—trustworthy.

With everyone making or saving money based on voluntary association, nine years later Airbnb is now valued at more than $20 billion. Hosts are happy, guests are happy, and investors are wealthy.

Who is not happy? Government regulators. They no longer get to define what's "safe" for us in the travel realm.

The Uber Revolution

When Travis Kalanick and Garrett Camp couldn't find a cab during a 2009 trip to Paris, they saw a system that was failing its consumers—and needed disruption.

According to the online magazine Techcrunch.com:

> Uber epitomizes disruption. The company has changed the way we think about grabbing a ride, incorporating the same technology we take for granted today into a brand new experience for consumers and an opportunity for producers.

Where Airbnb is rent sharing, Uber is ride sharing. And like Airbnb, Uber's value is in the trusted marketplace it created, providing the platform to connect people who need a ride with people who want to give them a ride, all without taxi unions and coordinated by a smartphone app. Circumventing antiquated monopolies on taxi service is the epitome of disruption, of delivering a product in a less expensive and more convenient way.

Gone are the days of hailing a taxi and fumbling with cash at the ride's end. The Uber app calls the car, shows its approach and arrival time, allows the rider to contact the driver, and makes the payment. Yet for all that convenience, Uber is usually less expensive than a cab.

But even if the price were identical, Uber's value surpasses traditional cab offerings with enhanced safety through driver ratings, the ability to share your trip online with friends, and the cashless nature of the app. As a woman who frequently travels alone, I use Uber almost exclusively, for safety reasons as well as for the convenience and control.

Millions of riders and drivers worldwide have found similar experiences. Only seven years after inception Uber is now valued at more than $50 billion.

Beneficial side effects beyond the direct value to riders and drivers exist alongside the financial successes. Both DUI arrests and DUI deaths decrease 3%-10% once Uber enters a market. When is the last time government reduced DUIs? Good business creates social good without the heavy-handed and intrusive force of government.

The Government Would Never Invent Any of This

Compare these technology successes to the failures when the federal government tries its hand. HealthCare.gov and the botched loan-guarantee scam of Solyndra come to mind, along with countless head-shaking boondoggles such as the infamous shrimp-on-a-treadmill study. When the government intrudes in business, trying to force its political agenda on an unforgiving marketplace, its ham-fisted blundering wastes trillions. With a T.

And its results are upside-down. Left to the government, inexpensive and popular LASIK would never have happened. As proof, look to the cost of medical care in general. Instead of widespread price-dropping innovations and breakthrough treatments, we see the opposite. If government control of medical care were effective, consumers would be lining up in droves outside Veteran's Administration hospitals. Instead, they regard those facilities as favorably as they would an army mess hall amid a cornucopia of trendy bistros.

Airbnb and Uber show that individuals and businesses thrive when doing business voluntarily with one another, outside of government interference. Entrenched hotel and taxicab companies may resent the competition, but they are free to innovate and find a business model that serves consumers even better.

They are even free to build on prior innovations, as Uber and Airbnb did. Both of those companies leveraged existing private-sector advancements, such as smartphones and PayPal, nurturing a relentless cascade of value that helps all levels of the economy. Consider how these two sharing services have helped the poor. Airbnb allows more people to travel more cheaply, and Uber not only saves riders money, it offers drivers an opportunity to supplement their income according to their own schedules. Ask your driver, as I have, how they like working for Uber. The stories are inspiring.

But imagine the government trying to spearhead disruptive business models, such as these peer-to-peer marketplaces. The wails of rent-seeking lodging and transportation lobbies would make the government hesitate. Toadying legislators voting to strengthen protectionist barriers would slow progress more. In the end, the disruption would never occur, killed by government caution, cronyism, and control.

Fixing the Problems Without Government

If the free market always does better, more efficient, and more useful work than the government, how can it help solve social problems? How can the examples of 3D printing, LASIK, Airbnb, and Uber inform us about how the private sector can help fix our Fireworks social issues? Can the free market do a better job than the government?

What should a person do who is opposed to abortion but who takes exception to the intrusive government snooping that would accompany restrictions? Or what about the person opposed to abortion who doesn't think that making it illegal would reduce the frequency?

What if someone feels called to reduce gun violence, but doesn't want the government restricting the rights of millions of law-abiding gun owners? Or what about the person who is personally opposed to guns but has concluded that gun bans don't reduce gun violence?

What should a person do whose heartstrings are pulled by the plight of children in underperforming schools, but who doesn't want the one-size-fits-all behemoth of a federal solution?

What if someone believes that same-sex marriage is undermining traditional marriage, but doesn't want the government intruding into anyone's personal relationships?

Private answers abound to each of these dilemmas, more effective than any government mandate, law, or regulation. As in the marketplace of commerce, motivated individuals acting voluntarily in the marketplace of ideas can succeed in ways the government cannot, making disruptive and enduring differences on consequential issues without resorting to the imposition and failures that accompany legislative "remedies."

CHAPTER 7

REDUCING ABORTIONS

E veryone cares.
On the topic of human life and its creation, everyone cares. And because of its profound moral implications, abortion is profoundly political. Those on the pro-life side *legitimately* believe they are saving unborn babies with their work. Those on the pro-choice side *legitimately* believe they are protecting vulnerable women from being trapped in untenable circumstances.

Perhaps new definitions are in order.

Incomplete Definitions

The traditional meanings for the oft-used terms "pro-life" and "pro-choice" are becoming inadequate.

Views among pro-life people vary considerably. Certain of them think that the only way to solve the problem of abortions is to make them illegal, and some of these pro-lifers further think that any attempt to prevent pregnancy, like birth control, should also be illegal. That doesn't describe all pro-life people. According to a 2014 Gallup poll, 89% of Republicans have no moral opposition to birth control. We can suppose that some of that remaining 11% with moral qualms about birth control wouldn't favor making it illegal for others.

Some pro-choice people think that unwanted pregnancies are the biggest barriers to women's success in life, and that terminating a pregnancy up to the moment before delivery is legal and moral. That doesn't describe all pro-choice people. According to a 2012 Gallup poll, only 14% of Americans support third-trimester abortions.

Yet many don't fit into either of those two categories. Personally, I would not have an abortion because I believe that a fetus is a human life. So, according to my morals, abortion is wrong. This makes me pro-life.

However, even though I want there to be fewer abortions, I don't want the government trying to accomplish this goal. The government ruins nearly everything it touches, which is why I don't want them to be the exclusive source of providing alternatives to abortion or education about it. And if banning abortion by overturning *Roe v. Wade* is likely to *increase* the number of abortions, that isn't a good solution either.

Since I don't want *Roe v. Wade* overturned, then does that make me pro-choice? Of course not. This is exactly why the definitions "pro-life" and "pro-choice" are so incomplete.

I'm coining a new term: Pro-Life Realist.

A pro-life realist is a person who, like me, desperately wants to decrease the number of abortions, and who is personally pro-life, but who also knows that making abortions illegal isn't the path to reducing them. Based on history and statistics, we see strong evidence that banning abortions is likely to lead to their *increase*.

We also see that free-market solutions, not the heavy-handed and ruinous touch of government, are reducing abortions. And that's reason for optimism.

What No One Wants

No one wants there to be more abortions.

There, I said it. No one wants there to be more abortions.

Whether a person is pro-choice or pro-life, there is no sane person who thinks that the world would be better if only there were more abortions. Before we move on, let's agree that everyone reading this page wants there to be fewer abortions.

If you think that this country needs to increase the number of abortions, please put this book down immediately and give it away. This book is not for you.

The salient question to explore is whether, to reduce abortions, it is more effective to use government or private means.

Legal Abortion Is Here to Stay

The reality is that *Roe v. Wade* is likely never going away. It has survived the pro-life presidencies of Ronald Reagan, George H. W. Bush, and George W. Bush, facing no serious threats even during those terms. Nor does the public favor abolishing it. A 2013 poll revealed that most Americans do not want to see *Roe v. Wade* overturned.

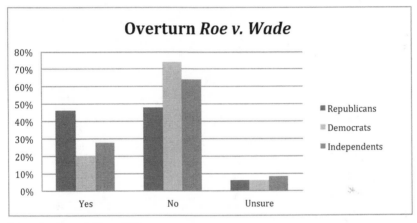

Source: Pew Research Center, 2013

Over time, public support for maintaining *Roe v. Wade* is only increasing.

There is no reason to imagine a reversal of this trend, but even if your hope is that Roe v. Wade may get overturned *someday*, it isn't going away *today*. So what can be done today that would help reduce the number of abortions?

Abortion Rates Are Low Because Birth Control Is Better

Although access to abortion has been legal for more than four decades, the incidence of abortion continues to decrease, and is at its lowest point

Consistent Support for Maintaining *Roe v. Wade* Over Past 20 Years

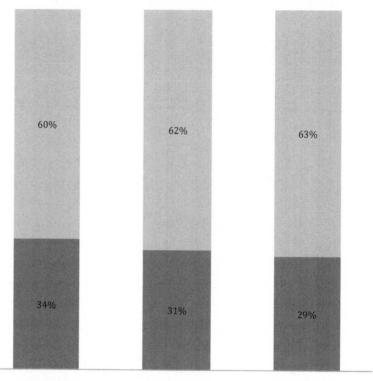

■ Completely overturn Roe v. Wade   ■ Not overturn Roe v. Wade

60%

62%

63%

34%

31%

29%

Source: Pew Research Center, 2013

since the 1973 landmark case. What would cause the rate of abortion to go down, even though ease of access is at unprecedented levels?

Better Information

Access to and quality of birth control has significantly improved over the decades. Women looking for the birth control pill in the 1960s tell stories of having to find a separate doctor to prescribe the pill, since their own family doctor didn't believe in birth control. Today, such a sentiment would be unheard of. And if there were a random doctor who didn't want to prescribe the pill today, there would be hundreds of other doctors available and willing to do so.

Social taboos against discussing birth control have effectively vanished. It is common to hear women of all ages discuss with each other the type of birth control they use, sharing advice on brands and compositions. With television commercials now extolling any particular brand's virtues, mainstream societal reproof has been overcome.

Some birth control pills have even been shown to clear up acne, reduce dysmenorrhea, and mitigate the symptoms of other conditions like polycystic ovary syndrome and endometriosis. Birth control, and specifically the birth control pill, is a mainstream medication, and laws are changing to acknowledge that. Since late 2015 both Oregon and California allow purchase directly from a pharmacist, without a prescription. National legislation has been proposed from both Republicans and Democrats to make this type of direct, over-the-counter access national.

Despite the scare tactics from certain political campaigns, *access to birth control is not at risk.*

Better Medicine

From its initial availability in 1957 to treat only severe menstrual disorders, the daily birth control pill has continued to improve. After three years of coincidental increase in women reporting severe menstrual disorders, it was approved in 1960 for contraceptive use. Advancements since then include gentler formulations, fewer side effects, and more flexibility for women.

These changes allow women who weren't previously able to tolerate the original formulations to take the pill. They allow nursing mothers to take the pill. And they provide options for women to menstruate once every three months, instead of once a month.

Better Marketplace

As adoption of birth control grew, the marketplace developed new methods, allowing women more choice than ever. In concert, more health insurance plans voluntarily covered these additional methods of birth control and permanent sterilization procedures. Even women who are uninsured or who cannot afford these medications, have convenient access to birth control. Planned Parenthood, for example, offers free birth control nationwide for those who can't afford it, including:

- Birth control pills
- Depo-Provera
- IUDs
- The Patch
- NuvaRing
- Emergency contraception
- Non-prescription products like male and female condoms and contraceptive gels
- Sterilization—both vasectomy and tubal ligation

All of these improvements have reduced the need for abortions through pregnancy prevention.

Yet every election season in swing districts sees renewed conversation about whether birth control is here to stay. Fringe groups use fear tactics to suggest that some candidate or policy risks birth control being banned. But to the dismay of a small handful of activists who want such a ban, access to inexpensive or free birth control, and the significant choices it gives to women, *is never going away*. Not in a culture where even 82% of Catholics polled say that birth control is morally acceptable.

Those who say that the legality of birth control is in jeopardy are mistaken.

An Image of Sanctity

There has also been a shift in the social acceptance of abortions. Gallup polls conducted in 1996 and 2014 showed the percentage of respondents who define themselves as pro-life *increasing* from 33% to 46%.

At a glance, a 13% increase in 18 years of people describing themselves as pro-life should be welcome news for people who want to reduce the number of abortions. But remember that 63% of respondents in the Pew Research poll do not want to see *Roe v. Wade* overturned, *which includes pro-life people*.

How can this be so? Who are these people who are pro-life and yet don't want existing law overturned? They are the people described earlier who, despite their own beliefs, don't want the government controlling decisions we make in our lives. They are the pro-life realists.

Consider a 20-year-old woman today. The first baby picture she ever saw of herself was the ultrasound from when she was still *in utero*. That picture has been on the refrigerator since she can remember, just like those of her siblings. Seeing that picture, she makes the subconscious mental leap that a fetus must be a human life, because her 20-year-old self is alive. But it doesn't mean that she wants to make abortion illegal. She is part of the trend away from letting government control our decisions.

Some in the pro-life activist community, who also don't think *Roe v. Wade* will ever be overturned, say that this battle is about changing hearts and minds. Technology is helping them.

But not when it's forced. Ten states *mandate* some form of ultrasound prior to getting an abortion. The notion is that upon seeing the ultrasound pictures, the woman will have a change of heart and keep her baby. But the indignity and coercion of capturing the ultrasound erase the benefits of any intended compassion. Many of these states demand the highest quality ultrasound, which at early pregnancy stages—when most abortions are performed—means not an external ultrasound, but a transvaginal one. This is exactly as invasive as it sounds.

And the result? A study in 2014 by the *Journal of Obstetrics and Gynecology* shows that when a woman has largely made up her mind to have an abortion, seeing the image of the fetus is not likely to change her mind. Conversely, when she chooses *of her own free will* to have an ultrasound, she is more likely to change her mind.

Government-mandated ultrasounds are not the answer.

One Step Away

An increasing number of Americans don't want abortion to be illegal, even though they consider themselves pro-life. Why? Could it be that Americans are concerned about others who might be in a much more difficult situation?

Nearly one-third of Americans are only one paycheck away from poverty. This also means that one-third of Americans are only one financial crisis away from poverty. For these families an illness, accident, uninsured death, major car repair, or job loss can be devastating.

We all know someone on this financial precipice, and feel deep empathy for anyone in such circumstances. The homeless, 3.5 million of them over the course of a year, increasingly families, exist in even more dire situations. Perhaps it's a woman and her children, fleeing an abusive home and sleeping in their car for a few nights, or a family on the street following a job loss that resulted in an eviction for a few months. The face of homelessness is changing in this economy, and everyone has heard the sad and scary stories.

Pro-life realists, who don't think outlawing abortion will reduce abortion, may be *both* pro-life *and* be against the government outlawing abortion. They can easily imagine a woman in a dire financial situation who has an unplanned pregnancy. They fear she could be living out of her car if she experiences just one more financial setback.

The empathy is real, and informs their preferences, *even though they are pro-life*. Among even those who are not generally political, this is a common reason for pro-life people to want abortion kept legal.

The False Dilemma of Morality Versus Compassion

Many people look at legal abortion in very fixed terms. Some on one side see legal abortion as a purely moral issue. Some on the other side view it as purely an issue of compassion for the woman involved. Must it be so contradictory?

Professional Activists

Professional activists seek to polarize. It's the nature of politics and of organizational dynamics, and the whole reason why any professional activist group exists.

In the abortion debate it's especially true, with thousands of professional activists arrayed on either side. On the pro-choice side, organizations include NARAL Pro-Choice America, National Abortion Federation, The Pro-Choice Action Network, and Planned Parenthood. On the pro-life side are organizations such as National Right To Life, Pro-Life Action League, Operation Rescue, and American Life League.

These professional activists use language different from each other, and different from that of average people. A pro-life activist says of the pro-choice movement, "They are baby killers," and "They are committing a sin against God," and "They have no respect for the sanctity of life."

A pro-choice activist spins things differently. Regarding the pro-life movement, she says, "They want to compel women to have children," and "They want women to be forced into back alley abortions," and "They don't want women to have access to birth control."

Elevated to the political arena, the argument becomes one of morality versus compassion, each claiming the ethical high ground by denigrating the other. An observer reading the opposing side's literature would think that pro-choice people think only about how they can kill more babies, and that pro-life people want only to force poor women in unfortunate situations to have unwanted children.

Ordinary people don't think this way about abortion.

A Universal Sadness

Most people aren't professional activists. Average, everyday people—whether pro-choice or pro-life—understand that the decision to get an abortion is a very difficult one that the woman would prefer not to have to make. Average, everyday people have normal, non-political jobs; they go to work every day, take their kids to school, socialize with friends, and go to ballet recitals. They do everything they can to *not* think about politics at all.

These average, everyday people have likely had a more typical brush with abortion. Perhaps they agonized through the decision personally. Perhaps they talked someone out of an abortion. Perhaps they drove a friend to the clinic and held her through the tears.

What these average, everyday people know is that *none of these scenarios involving an abortion is ever happy.* Each one is sad, heartrending, and devastating. It may have involved a pregnant minor. It may have been a woman in an abusive relationship. It may have been a woman in an impossible financial situation.

These experiences are never joyful.

A woman never talks about how great her abortion experience was. She never talks about how she wants all her friends to have an abortion. She never talks about how she can't wait to have her next abortion. Never. *That isn't how it works.*

Even if a woman felt the decision to have an abortion was the right one at the time given her situation, the circumstances surrounding her abortion were exceedingly distressing—because of a bad relationship, financial distress, or family pressure.

From reading the talking points of professional activists—pro-choice and pro-life—you would think they no longer have a connection to these real people and real stories. Professional activists look at abortion as political calculus. It isn't political calculus to the real woman going through this difficult decision, whose real-life story is sadness and angst.

I don't think these real women are personally swayed by the pro-life and pro-choice political rhetoric.

A woman who has had an abortion, and feels that it was the right decision at the time, isn't likely to be moved by pictures of aborted fetuses, such as those on pro-life rally signs. A woman who has had an abortion and feels guilty about the decision will only feel worse seeing that sign. No hearts or minds are moved.

That same woman might not connect with any pro-choice message either. An appeal to women's empowerment and reproductive freedom likely doesn't comport with her reflection on her personal profound sadness.

Mass messages miss the point: these experiences are personal.

An Array of Alternatives

There are choices.

There are.

Crisis Pregnancy Centers

Approximately 2,500 crisis pregnancy centers operate in the U.S., both locally managed and branches of national organizations. Pro-life religious organizations operate most of them. They provide financial support and counseling to women who want to take a pregnancy to term, whether to raise a child, or to give a baby for adoption. Many centers provide adoption services themselves or work closely with area agencies.

Some crisis pregnancy centers have been criticized for trying to talk women out of abortion, for deceptive advertising that suggests they do abortions, and for imposing their religious views on vulnerable women. Abortion providers are equally disparaged: for trying to talk women into abortion, for minimizing risks, and for misleading patients about fetal development.

Fraudulent claims notwithstanding, each provider is selling a service. Abortion providers sell abortions. Crisis pregnancy centers sell birth, which includes trying to talk women out of abortions. Each service is legal, and thus permitted—even expected—to advertise, promote, and speak out against the other's business model.

But too often those speaking out spend their money counterproductively. Millions of dollars in political contributions are spent every year on both sides of the issue, with pro-choice groups always outspending pro-life groups. These contributions go directly to candidates who espouse the views of each side, and to other "soft-money" advertising efforts.

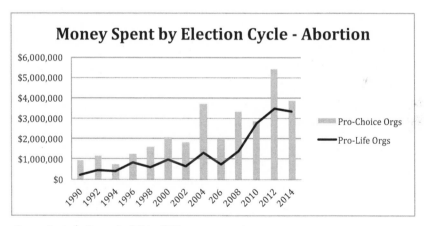

Source: *Center for Responsive Politics, 2014*

What if all of the time, energy, and money pro-life activists currently spend trying to make abortion illegal were instead spent on these types of crisis pregnancy centers?

What if a pregnant woman had a place to live and attend school and work during her pregnancy, where she was not made to feel ashamed of her choice to keep her baby?

What if she could meet face to face with birth mothers who gave their children up for adoption, some of whom remain happy with that choice and others who share the heartrending difficulties of their choice? She could also talk to birth mothers who decided to keep their babies, and understand the implications, joys, and difficulties of that decision.

What if she wants to keep her baby, but her family or the baby's father wants her to have an abortion?

What if the pregnant woman needs skills and support to raise her baby?

And what if the pro-life community came together, privately and without government intervention, to help in these circumstances? Is the rate of abortion likely to go up or down?

Pregnant women would have more options. Keeping a baby from an unplanned pregnancy would also be easier. Carrying a baby to term for adoptive parents might not be so difficult financially. For a woman looking for an easy solution, the process to continue a pregnancy might be as easy as the process to terminate one.

Between 1% and 4% of women with unwanted pregnancies choose adoption over abortion. Even more women might choose adoption if the process were easier. If they knew they could select the adoptive parents, or have their medical expenses covered, would that make a difference?

How could it not?

Voluntary Technology

Innovative organizations are using technology to change hearts and minds, and they are doing it voluntarily. The non-profit organization Save the Storks was founded by a group of concerned millennials who cite that 84% of women who have had an abortion *thought that it was their only choice.*

Because crisis pregnancy centers couldn't be everywhere, Save the Storks put the pregnancy center on wheels. The mobile unit—a Stork Bus, they call it—carries an ultrasound machine and a crisis pregnancy counselor. Three of five women who board the Stork Bus choose to keep their babies.

This is voluntary, *not mandated by the government.*

This private organization has nothing to do with forced ultrasounds that some states mandate, but rather increases the likelihood of a pregnant girl having the option of a voluntary ultrasound.

What about the other two of five who don't choose to keep their babies? Are they berated? According to Save the Storks, "The women who don't are never shamed or rejected because they choose abortion. Instead, they're assured that if they ever need future assistance, counseling, prayer, or support, that the people at the pregnancy center that operates the Stork Bus will be there for them."

Save the Storks acknowledges the political barriers facing their model of pregnancy resource centers (PRCs), and promotes individual, voluntary action to counteract them. According to Chris McIntire, their Chief Advancement Officer:

> The work of pro-life policy makers is critical because we have seen how the other side uses laws and regulations to inhibit the practices and innovations of PRCs. In California for example (where we have several Stork Buses), pro-abortion politicians are currently working with Planned Parenthood to pass legislation that, if successful, would severely limit, if not end, the ability for PRCs to function in a life-saving role.
>
> But for far too long the prerequisite for being pro-life was to vote for pro-life candidates every two years. Part of our mission is to help people realize that they don't need to wait for laws to change before taking action within their communities to help mothers and their unborn babies. The repeal of *Roe v. Wade* would not end the abortion crisis, and we believe that pro-life is not a left vs. right political issue . . . it's a justice issue.

For pro-life activists who have concluded that *Roe v. Wade* is settled law, but who still want to reduce the number of abortions, a private group like Save the Storks is a way to help.

Enough Love to Go Around

Not all children needing homes are newborns. Shouldn't the pro-life community care about those shuffled around the foster care system, or born into abusive or drug-addicted homes? Adopting children at any age, according to the pro-life movement, is about the culture of life and the culture of a stable family structure, and that's the sentiment needing promotion.

Based in Colorado Springs, Focus on the Family describes itself as "a global Christian ministry dedicated to helping families thrive." In 2008, they began partnering with churches in Colorado Springs, Ft. Lauderdale, Los Angeles, and St. Louis to place children from the foster care system into adoptive homes through adoption fairs. In all, 830 families started their adoption process at these sponsored events.

Given the success of these private adoption fairs, why aren't they everywhere? Because government regulations get in the way. To hold these fairs, Focus on the Family had to obtain exemptions from numerous laws governing the process. Put in place ostensibly to protect children, the onerous legal barriers instead impede the process of creating families, a social tragedy especially when there is enough love to go around.

Private answers from resolute communities can alleviate social problems even when government solutions stand in the way. As one activist told me, "Every life is precious, whether a newborn or a teenager. The pro-life community needs to put its money, and its heart, where its mouth is, and make sure all of these kids have a home."

When Abortions Are Outlawed...

What would life look like in the U.S. if abortions were outlawed? How would the law even be enforced? We can look across the globe to see. Ninety-one countries currently outlaw abortion, some making exceptions for the life of the mother and some not.

Although tracking abortions in countries where they are illegal can be difficult, trends nonetheless emerge.

Where abortions are illegal, more abortions occur.

The Guttmacher Institute compiles a significant amount of data on abortions worldwide. For purposes of comparing abortions in countries where abortion is illegal against countries where abortion is legal, consider Guttmacher's measurement *the number of abortions per 1,000 women aged 15-44*. Using this number, the differences become clear.

In the United States, that number is 16.9%, a comparatively low number that has been declining since the *Roe v. Wade* Supreme Court decision.

The Guttmacher Institute also tracks worldwide trends using this same measurement. In regions where abortion is illegal, the contrast is startling. In Latin America, where abortion remains illegal in many countries, the average rate is 32%. In Africa, where many countries also restrict abortion, the rate is 29%. It's also important to note that these high numbers *may actually be underreported*, as many illegal abortions may never be documented.

For those who believe that a legal ban on abortions would reduce the number of abortions, the comparison between countries with access to legal abortion and countries without access to legal abortions is instructive. If their actual goal is to reduce the number of abortions performed, then international trends indicate that a ban is the completely wrong answer. Additionally, no evidence supports the contention that state-level restrictions such as waiting periods, ultrasounds, and prohibitions after a specified number of weeks reduce the number of abortions.

In the United States, where access to legal abortion has been in effect since 1973, the rate of abortion has gone down—while it has been legal.

Certain staunchly pro-life organizations in the U.S. aim to end abortion by overturning *Roe v. Wade*. If those organizations acknowledged that making abortion illegal increases the incidence of abortion, might they adopt a new strategy? Might they want to look instead at methods that actually have a history of leading to a reduction in abortions?

Anti-Political Solutions

Although the government ruins nearly everything it touches, that doesn't stop activists from trying to exploit the politics of pull. Think of the uncountable millions—even hundreds of millions—spent every year on campaign contributions, lobbying, and media to influence abortion politics.

And yet for all that spending, nothing changes. Abortion is still legal, even as its incidence keeps declining. The number of abortions is at its lowest rate since the 1973 decision.

What if instead those dollars were spent to house pregnant teens through their third trimester, or to privately fund free birth control for at-risk women?

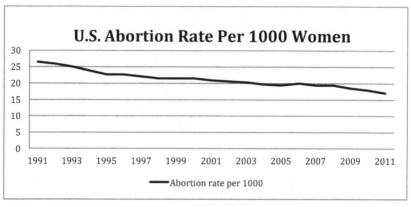

U.S. Abortion Rate Per 1000 Women

— Abortion rate per 1000

Source: Guttmacher Report: Abortion Incidence and Service Availability in the United States, 2011

Fellow pro-life realists, seeking actual reductions in abortions rather than misguided symbolism, would acknowledge that helping women in crisis situations achieves their goals more effectively than trying to overturn *Roe v. Wade*. At the very least they would stop wasting time and energy on political answers.

The politicians themselves could make the biggest difference. Imagine the most popular pro-life politicians agreeing to endorse every pro-life organization in their legislative districts, promoting fundraising and awareness events. With more privately raised funds, these organizations could help reduce the number of abortions performed, and all without government intrusion into our private decisions.

Those politicians would be pro-life realists in action, modeling behavior for their constituents, who themselves were previously frustrated pro-life activists. Seeing political leaders promote non-political answers would encourage citizens to do the same, to give their time to groups that help reduce abortions privately.

A person can be pro-life, and believe
that the government can't reduce abortions.

Politicians who adopt anti-political solutions to abortion would also free their legislative time to improve jobs and the economy. And in a better economy, fewer women would seek abortions as an answer to their financial distress.

Courageous anti-political politicians and pro-life realists in action could accomplish the ends they espouse, if their focus were more on solutions and less on sanctimony.

Fund Abortion and Crisis Pregnancy Centers Privately

Two key political discussion points surface in any debate concerning abortion.

The first centers on its legality: timeframes and exceptions for rape, incest, and the life of the mother. The second is funding: Who should pay?

Hyde and Seek

Immediately after the 1973 *Roe v. Wade* decision, abortion was privately funded, a cash-on-delivery procedure. A social-conscience push arose soon after, to publicly fund abortions for the poor.

In 1976 the Hyde Amendment passed, prohibiting the use of Health and Human Services (HHS) funds for abortions. A rider to the HHS budget, the Hyde Amendment continues to be attached to many current pieces of legislation. The pro-life community sees this as an ongoing victory, understandably not wanting their tax dollars to pay for abortions. More than half of Americans share this view.

In 2014 Planned Parenthood, the nation's largest provider of women's health services, including abortions, received $540 million in federal funding, about half of their annual budget. Planned Parenthood performs one out of every four abortions in the U.S., but according to the Hyde Amendment, no federal dollars can directly fund these procedures. Nonetheless, federal funding can be used to pay for education and other efforts, which Planned Parenthood insists is how the financial ledgers align. Pro-life activists scoff at the accounting, recognizing that dollars used for education free up money to provide abortions.

Ending government funding for abortion providers removes one of the stumbling blocks in the pro-life community. And it causes Planned Parenthood and similar groups to raise private funds to support those in financial need.

Keep Crisis Pregnancy Centers Private

Although many crisis pregnancy centers are privately funded, some receive state and federal subsidies. Some funds came from Obama's 2009 Recovery Act, some through state health departments, and some through the National Fatherhood Initiative. Not everyone supports this use of public money, especially to religious institutions.

Pro-life activists don't want their tax dollars paying for abortions.

Pro-choice activists don't want their tax dollars paying for crisis pregnancy centers.

Both sides are expressing Thomas Jefferson's truism: "To compel a man to furnish contributions of money for the propagation of opinions which he disbelieves and abhors, is sinful and tyrannical." That sinful tyranny is why Planned Parenthood (and similar organizations) should be privately funded and crisis pregnancy centers should *also* be privately funded. We should listen to our third president and get the government out of funding either side.

A Private Responsibility

According to a 2014 CBS News poll, greater than half of Americans say that regardless of their own personal stance on the issue, it is wrong for the government to pay for abortions. Yet the Democratic Party platform supports a woman's access to abortion, "regardless of her ability to pay." This is out of step with the majority of Americans.

Is it possible that Planned Parenthood could replace its taxpayer funding with additional private fundraising? Supporters of access to free birth control and abortion could donate privately, just as pro-life activists could privately support crisis pregnancy centers. In its 2012–2013 annual report, Planned Parenthood reported that roughly 50% of its revenue came from federal funding, with 23% from "Non-Government Health Services," and 26% from "Private Contributions and Bequests." This indicates willingness for people to privately support low cost access to birth control and abortion.

Are the two-thirds of Americans who do not want to see *Roe v. Wade* overturned willing to put their money where their heart is and donate privately to provide universal access to legal abortions?

Those concerned about the plight of poor women with unplanned pregnancies could help them directly and privately, funding either abortion providers or pregnancy centers, as their own morals dictate. Consider how much time, effort, and money would be freed up if abortion were no longer the political football it is today.

Improve Adoption

Estimates place the number of American couples waiting to adopt between 600,000 and 1,000,000. Yet every day, many of them become frustrated with domestic red tape and decide to adopt internationally.

In the post-World War II era, the practice of adopting children from war-torn and poverty-stricken countries became more prominent. Today that practice continues, and it should. Without question, overseas crises pull at the heartstrings of adoptive American parents, and for those called to humanitarian purpose the rewards can be substantial. But it's a disservice to underserved children in this country when adoptive parents turn to international rescue only because the process for domestic adoptions is prohibitive.

Support Choice in Adoption

Regardless of whether a child is adopted internationally or domestically, if the process were significantly easier, it's apparent that there wouldn't be *more* abortions. And one barrier to domestic adoptions is a set of "non-discrimination" laws that restrict an agency's ability to select parents who believe as they do. These laws insert government between children who want a "forever home" and adoptive parents.

Catholic Charities has been providing adoption services since 1902, and prefers to place children in two-parent traditional marriage homes. That should be its right. The Jewish Children Adoption Network places a high value on Jewish children being adopted by Jewish families.

The government should not stop them. Laws that don't allow for placement choice, whether for religious or other reasons, should be repealed.

These or other adoption agencies, religious or otherwise, that don't want to place children with same-sex couples or single parents, shouldn't be forced by law to do so. Keeping government out of these decisions clears the way for adoption agencies that specialize in same-sex couples looking to adopt, and for birth parents seeking that option.

Dictating how an agency selects the most loving and compatible families is not the proper role of government. Instead, adoption agencies, adoptive parents, and birth mothers should convene to make decisions for the best outcome for the child.

Integrate Insurance

Although most insurance covers medical expenses for adoptive children, very few cover the pre-natal and maternity expenses for the birth mother. Most birth mothers who are uninsured must instead use Medicaid or state programs that cover low-income individuals.

When the adoptive parents support the birth mother through her pregnancy, insurers should consider offering them policies that cover a non-related birth mother. Knowing that her medical coverage would be convenient and high quality might make it easier for the birth mother to choose adoption.

Leverage Compassion

Since the government ruins nearly everything it touches, we can do better than ask them to reduce the number of abortions, especially since government bans have proved counterproductive.

Instead, we serve our neighbors best when we leverage our own compassion, choosing as private citizens to extend a hand, a heart, and a home to mothers in need.

CHAPTER 8

LESS GUN VIOLENCE

Most people want less crime, and want fewer criminals using guns to commit those crimes. But even reasonable, well-intentioned people disagree on how to make it happen.

Gun control advocates think that reducing the overall availability of firearms aids this goal, while gun rights advocates believe instead that a well-armed citizenry is the best way to reduce gun violence.

There's more. Each of the Fireworks issues carries emotional weight, and gun control is no different, eliciting visceral responses from all sides. Gun ownership and use are among the most enduring American traditions, and those who advocate for more gun rights have been known to challenge anyone to pry their guns from their cold, dead hands. Conversely, gun control advocates see the human misery of guns used for violence, of children and innocents dying, and cry that *something must be done*. Emotions run high.

But emotions notwithstanding, one agreement remains: everyone wants gun violence reduced.

Gun Control Laws Don't Reduce Gun Violence

The data on gun control is clear.

There has never been a gun control law
that reduced gun crime. Never.

The facts show the opposite is true. Where gun control is the most restrictive, gun-related crimes increase. Consider that Washington, D.C. and Chicago both have among the strictest gun control laws in the nation, and yet own the highest levels of gun crime. Historically, when stricter gun controls are enacted, gun crime increases. The reason? Law-abiding citizens follow the new law. Criminals don't.

In 1965, 40% of the murders in Chicago were committed using handguns. In 1982, when their city council voted 30 to 11 to ban handguns, 43% of murders committed in Chicago were committed using handguns. By 2007, that rate was 79%. The handgun ban didn't work.

Nor do laws limiting magazine size. Imagine a criminal preparing to rob a store, and considering which gun magazine to use. Would knowing that a larger, more effective magazine is illegal affect his choice? Of course not. Having already elected to commit armed robbery, he won't be deterred by the prospect of breaking additional laws. That's the funny thing about criminals. They commit crimes.

Suppose further that upon approaching the store, the criminal noticed that it was within a designated gun-free zone. Would he stop short, abandoning his plans because he discovered that guns were not allowed? Never happen.

But a law-abiding citizen would act differently. Someone with a legal concealed carry permit is far more likely to respect the wishes of a business that wants to be gun free. She is also more likely to respect a restriction on gun magazine size if the law demands.

But if laws and signs won't deter gun crime, what will? What do criminals fear?

They fear dying.

Which is why they fear an armed citizen more than they fear the police. An armed citizen could be anywhere, while law enforcement officers stand out. Aside from undercover and plain-clothes officers, members of law enforcement are intentionally easy to spot, so criminals steer clear. Even the densest criminal knows that law enforcement officers carry guns.

Evidence for the failure of gun control laws is not just anecdotal. Many studies—and not only those from traditionally pro-gun rights organizations—agree that gun laws don't reduce gun crime. A 2007 Harvard University research paper titled, "Would Banning Firearms Reduce Murder and Suicide?" which covered the U.S. and parts of Europe, concluded simply:

"Stricter laws don't mean there is less crime."

A 1994 study by Duke University, "Ten Myths About Gun Control," found that:

> "No empirical study of the effectiveness of gun laws has shown any positive effect on crime."

More gun laws don't reduce gun violence.

The Tide of Public Opinion Is Turning

As more data is becoming available on the correlation between responsible gun ownership and the reduction of crime—especially gun crime—public opinion is changing. Gun ownership has become much more mainstream, and gun rights discussions occur during political discussions in the public square.

An October 2015 CNN poll showed that more than half of Americans oppose stricter gun control laws, with a 52% to 46% margin. Just four months prior, sentiment was equally split at 49% each.

Professional organizations representing both sides parallel the public divide. Let's acknowledge that guns will always exist in America, and that reducing crime is the common goal of all groups. Not the elimination of guns. Not arming every citizen. Neither confiscation nor conscription, but reasonable policies whose aim is protecting our citizenry.

The existence of guns in America is integral to our culture. Though we can't know exactly, there are perhaps 310 million privately owned firearms in America, with up to 10 million guns added each year. If the country made guns illegal today, alongside some nationwide collection and confiscation policy, the authorities could never round up all those guns. A gun-free America is not logistically possible.

Gun ownership in America will never go away. No magic wands will whisk all the weapons elsewhere. The option is simply unavailable.

If you think that guns have no place in American society and believe that it is possible to confiscate all of them, put this book down immediately. It is not for you.

Those who acknowledge that guns are here to stay, and who want everyone with guns to be as safe as possible, can partake of the meaningful discussion.

Apples to Apples

Gun violence means a specific thing. It means that someone with a gun intends to harm an innocent person by using that gun. Without this consistent definition, there can be no fair statistical comparisons. Gun violence is not legal hunting, military use, mere ownership, using a firearm for defense of self or others, or any other use of a firearm that does not constitute a crime.

The distinction is important, because gun control organizations use different definitions to inflate crime statistics. To explore reducing gun violence, we're considering only actual gun violence.

Using that consistent definition, gun crime is decreasing in America. According to the FBI's statistics, gun crimes and violent crimes are down in the last 20 years.

During roughly that same period, gun ownership increased dramatically. The number of privately owned firearms in America increased from 192 million in 1994 to 310 million in 2009.

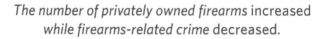

The number of privately owned firearms increased while firearms-related crime decreased.

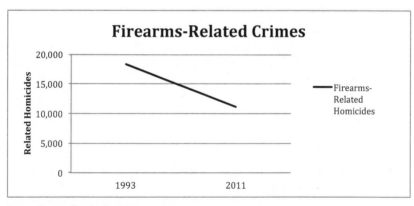

Source: Bureau of Justice Statistics

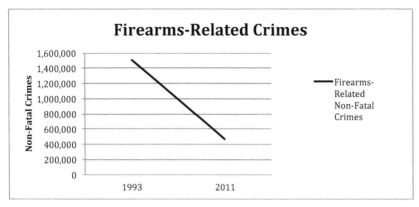

Source: Bureau of Justice Statistics

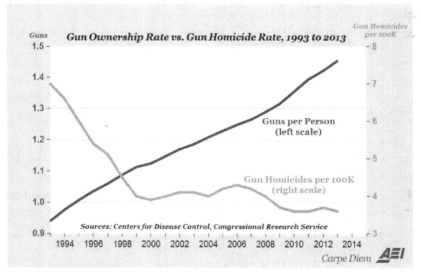

Reprinted with permission http://www.aei.org/publication/chart-of-the-day-more-gun
s-less-gun-violence-between-1993-and-2013/

Given that gun violence is decreasing, which policies will accelerate
that trend and which will hinder it?

Gun-Free Zones Become Defense-Free Zones

In a gun-free zone, whether a school, retail establishment, or movie theater, firearms are banned. Surface logic suggests that such zones ought to be effective in reducing gun violence: in order to stop shootings, prohibit the possession of any firearm.

Human nature renders the gun-free zone designation ironic at least, and dangerous at worst.

Mayhem Is Already Illegal

A shooter on a school campus, for example, intends to hurt or kill. Those acts are already illegal. How can a paper prohibition on guns on campus possibly deter someone who plans and commits homicide?

Sitting Ducks

In a gun-free zone, the person intent on doing harm expects no armed response to his shooting. As the only one armed, the criminal within those boundaries feels safer—which is why mass shootings happen there. The Crime Prevention Research Center finds that "since 2009, only 8% of mass public shootings have occurred in places where citizens are allowed to defend themselves."

In many mass public shootings, the shooter has carefully planned out the attack, including selecting a gun-free zone. The shooter in the Aurora, Colorado theater shooting bypassed six other theaters on the way to his kill zone, each showing the same Batman movie, and one of which boasted the largest auditorium in the area. But all six of those allowed concealed carry. His destination did not.

Criminals view a gun-free zone designation as a welcome mat.

An Invisible Army

Where guns are allowed, law-abiding citizens retract that mat.

Even in the same Chicago whose three-decade handgun ban—a *de jure* gun-free zone—actually increased gun violence, the perception of a defenseless citizenry can change.

In April 2015, from the seat of his Uber cab, a driver saw Everardo Custodio open fire into a crowd in Logan Square. A mass shooting was underway, with multiple casualties imminent. The driver drew his concealed carry firearm, legal only since a 2010 Supreme Court decision overturned Chicago's local handgun ban, and fired six shots at Custodio, wounding him in the thigh, shin, and lower back.

Custodio fell to the ground, incapacitated and bleeding. Countless Chicagoans Custodio could have killed continued to breathe.

The driver stayed on the scene to assist police when they finally arrived.

The law-abiding driver, acting in defense of himself and others, was not charged. Everardo Custodio has been sentenced to prison on weapons charges.

The message to others: an area where citizens can protect themselves is safer for the public, and is the worst place for criminals to be.

Which Stranger Do You Trust?

Are you uncomfortable imagining your neighbors or your cab drivers carrying concealed firearms? You are not alone. Many people distrust an armed citizenry around them, and it makes sense to be on your guard with your safety and your family's safety at stake.

Consider whether it makes you *more* uncomfortable imagining your friends and neighbors carrying concealed firearms than to think about a criminal with evil intent carrying a firearm. It is a certainty that the criminal will obtain a gun, carry it, and use it for illegal ends, regardless of how you feel or what some statute says. For confirmation, just turn on the nightly news.

Strangers with guns are a cause for ease, not alarm.

A 2014 study by the Crime Prevention Center showed that 11.1 million Americans have permits to carry a concealed handgun. This number has more than doubled in seven years, from 4.5 million in 2007. During that same period, the Department of Justice reported that murder and violent crime rates dropped by 22%.

Mathematically, 4.5% of all American adults have a concealed carry permit, but the incidence of crime—especially gun crime—among this group is tiny. Not all states record whether a suspect has a concealed carry permit, but those that do show that concealed carry permit holders are about 14 times *less likely* to commit a crime and five times less likely to commit a violent crime than those without.

> *Concealed carry holders are more law*
> *abiding than the average citizen.*

In a 2013 PoliceOne survey of 15,000 law enforcement officers, 91% said concealed carry should be permitted to citizens "without question and without further restrictions." Front-line officers, those who have the greatest personal insight on gun crimes and gun violence, trust concealed carry permit holders.

When considering who to trust regarding the safety of your family, recognize that concealed carry permit holders commit fewer crimes, and by their presence deter more crimes, than the general population. Concerns to the contrary are unsubstantiated by facts.

"Assault" Rifle or "Defense" Rifle?

Gun control advocates commonly assert that the only use for a semi-automatic rifle (or "assault rifle" as many call it) is to commit mass murder. Dianne Feinstein, U.S. Senator from California, said, "I have no problem with people being licensed and buying a firearm. But these [semi-automatic rifles] are weapons that you are only going to be using to kill people in close combat." Richard Blumenthal, U.S. Senator from Connecticut, said that such weapons are "primarily for criminal purposes," and it was "simply appropriate" to ban them.

However, examples abound of business owners, faced with civil unrest, using precisely that type of rifle to defend their businesses from looting. In the 1992 Los Angeles riots, Richard Rhee, a Korean War veteran and supermarket owner, shouldered such a rifle to defend his business from being looted and razed. "Burn this down after 33 years? They don't know how hard I've worked," he said. "This is my market and I'm going to protect it."

John Chu, vacationing in Los Angeles when the riots erupted, rushed to help Rhee defend the California Market. "Where are the police? Where are the soldiers?" he asked.

While looting was rampant in surrounding Los Angeles, Rhee and other store owners and supporters in Koreatown, well-armed with shotguns and semi-automatic rifles, defended their property from violent, roving bands of looters, even as adjacent neighborhoods burned to the ground.

Richard Rhee in Los Angeles and an Uber driver in Chicago are not alone. All over the country, armed citizens, usually concealed carry holders, have stopped violent crimes. These stories usually don't make the evening news, but the statistics are instructive.

Bureau of Justice Statistics report that between 1987 and 1992 62,000+ victims each year used a firearm defensively. Gary Kleck, criminology professor from Florida State University, found an even higher number in his National Self-Defense Survey. Kleck determined that from 1988 to 1993, 2.3 million Americans each year defended themselves with firearms. Not all of the incidents involved firing a weapon; in many cases, merely displaying one stops a crime. Countless defensive uses of firearms go unreported because a crime doesn't happen in these instances.

Fewer Guns or Fewer Crimes?

Examples from around the country shed more light on the issue. Washington, D.C. has the highest rate of murders and gun-related robberies in America. Yet for more than 30 years, the District boasted the strictest gun control in the country, including banning any new firearms and requiring existing guns to be disassembled and locked away at home.

Although the Supreme Court struck down the gun ban in 2008, during D.C.'s 30 years of strict gun control and beyond, criminals rampaged, knowing they would never encounter an armed citizen. Lawbreakers know that even now it is largely illegal to carry concealed in Washington, D. C., and the numbers reflect it: violent crime in the nation's capital in 2013 was three times worse than the national average.

Conversely, the cities with the lowest rates of gun crime have among the least strict gun control laws. According to the CATO Institute:

> The 31 states that have "shall issue" laws allowing private citizens to carry concealed weapons have, on average, a 24 percent lower violent crime rate, a 19 percent lower murder rate and a 39 percent lower robbery rate than states that forbid concealed weapons. In fact, the nine states with the lowest violent crime rates are all right-to-carry states.

Proponents of gun control need to answer this question honestly: Do they want to eliminate private ownership of guns, or do they want to reduce gun violence? Just as those are two different questions, the two answers are different.

Anti-Political Solutions

Government ruins nearly everything. Their gun control laws have never reduced gun crime, their gun-free zones become invitations for violence, and their knee-jerk answer to mass shootings is to look for ways to restrict the ability of law-abiding citizens to defend themselves.

For a person who wants to reduce gun violence—and this includes gun control advocates who have acknowledged that guns will never go away in America—what can be done?

The proper solutions for this and other Fireworks issues are private and anti-political.

Treat Firearms Like Cars

Both firearms and cars are tools used by millions of Americans. When operated inappropriately, either can kill. Intentionally or otherwise, drunk or sober, drivers have mowed down pedestrians, injured police officers, and driven through walls, landing in living rooms like a stray bullet. When people misuse these machines, innocents die.

Even families without swimming pools teach their children to swim. We lecture our children about stranger danger so that they won't be abducted. We instruct our children to dial 911 in an emergency. Why would we leave out a major category of safety training? Should we live in denial, not believing that our kids will ever encounter guns?

Some gun control advocates reject this comparison. They want to believe that the only purpose for a gun is to kill people. But approximately 45 million people in the U.S. hunt, including more than 3 million women. More than 16 million people regularly participate in shooting sports. Many millions more quietly carry concealed, or have a firearm in the home for self-defense that has never seen use, but instead acts as an insurance policy.

The gun control community worries that promoting or teaching gun safety will glamorize guns, but our culture does this already. The only question is whether that attraction leads to safe encounters or unsafe ones.

Overlook Ownership Legalities

Guns are serious tools that can hurt people, and anyone who could possibly be around them should be trained to be safe. This includes people who own guns illegally.

News stories abound of children who accidently shoot someone after finding a parent's firearm, some of which are illegally owned. Perhaps the parent stored the gun irresponsibly, perhaps the child defeated the safety feature, perhaps he didn't understand the danger.

How do those families get needed safety training? Gang members and other criminals might be reluctant to seek training, but doesn't a gang member's little brother deserve protection? Imagine a class held in an inner city that instructed gun owners how to store their firearms safely. Class organizers could choose to ignore whether any gun was legally owned, being concerned only with reducing accidents. Is it likely that safety classes would increase or decrease gun accidents?

Accepting the reality of an illegal circumstance, and choosing to mitigate the consequences, is the model successfully used in needle exchange programs across the country. The drugs participants use in such programs are illegal, but the program sponsors accept that reality, and choose nonetheless to protect addicts from the additional burdens of diseases such as Hepatitis C and HIV.

Following this model, gun safety advocates should promote safe firearm usage, regardless of whether the guns are legally or illegally owned.

Promote Competition

Many decades ago, public schools taught gun safety. High schools had rifle teams alongside their basketball and football teams. It was as common then to see a teenager with a rifle in his car, as it is now to see a student transporting her lacrosse equipment.

Picture a high school rifle team getting off the school bus after having traveled across town for a rival match: a bus full of teenagers with rifles slung across their shoulders—and no one batting an eye. In that era, homicide rates were about half of what they are today.

High school gun clubs are slowly making a comeback. In Minnesota, for example, their State High School Clay Target League's mission is:

> To attract students in grades six through twelve to participate in shooting sports while creating a friendly competition among high schools throughout Minnesota.

Friendly competition for ages 10 to 18. With guns.

Advocates of cultural inclusivity argue that learning promotes acceptance—that we fear what we don't understand. These teenagers learn and understand shooting, so they can accept each other, and guns, without fear.

Take It Outdoors

John Annoni saves at-risk youth. In the high-crime community of Allentown, Pennsylvania, his Camp Compass Academy takes urban kids out of the classroom and into the woods.

Its mission since 1994:

> Camp Compass is a unified effort to introduce urban, middle & high school students to various outdoor activities." These activities include "hunting, fishing, archery, tutoring, social guidance, and other outdoor youth activities" which are taught by John's volunteer mentors.

Participants are urban students, many growing up without the parental care that shapes a responsible, respectful, and productive adult. Missing a family structure at home, they often turn to gangs for acceptance. Through Camp Compass Academy, Annoni is stepping in before the gangs can get a foothold.

One day each week, 30 students from grades 6 to 12 learn outdoor skills, gun safety, and respect. Annoni teaches that guns are tools, no different than hammers—both useful and dangerous. The forbidden mystique of firearms evaporates, as participants spend hours planning the hunting trips that highlight each season.

Annoni, a middle-school teacher, founded Camp Compass Academy because his classroom time was not enough to teach the skills his students needed to break the cycle of crime trapping so many of them. Gun safety was a by-product.

Many parents started off skeptical at the idea of sending their inner-city children into the woods, armed. They wondered whether kids taught gun safety as if it were drivers' safety might be more likely to commit a crime with a firearm.

Results clearly say not.

Annoni proudly points out that for the program's 20-year history:

"We've never had a program participant involved in any gun crime."

Through Camp Compass Academy, John Annoni is making a difference *privately*. "We're saving lives," he says, and every Academy participant who chooses not to join a gang is living proof.

Add a Little History

Two national organizations build on our nation's history, creating character at the intersection of tradition and marksmanship.

The Boy Scouts of America are history in action. Since the organization's inception in 1910, it has offered a marksmanship badge, with firearms safety one of its criteria. No scout achievement is won in a vacuum; each is earned under the aegis of the Scout Oath, with its most potent directive, "to help other people at all times."

Less well known—but with chapters in every state—is Project Appleseed, a nonprofit organization that uses rifle training to teach history and civics. A 100% volunteer project of the Revolutionary War Veterans Association, Project Appleseed is "dedicated to teaching every American our shared heritage and history as well as traditional rifle marksmanship skills."

Why teach shooting skills in a project with a historical focus? According to Project Appleseed:

> Because good shooting requires learning positive traits such as patience, determination, focus, attention to detail, and persistence. Since

these skills are likewise key elements of mature participation in civic activities, we urge our students to take what they have learned about themselves as marksmen and apply it to their participation in their communities and in the wider American society.

At the very least, these programs teach their participants not only marksmanship, but also the very anti-political notions of self-reliance and civic responsibility.

Teach Four Steps

In 2013, there were 505 accidental firearms deaths, some of them children. Although considerably fewer than car accidents and drowning, this is still too many. How many more children would be alive if gun safety were the norm today, and not the exception?

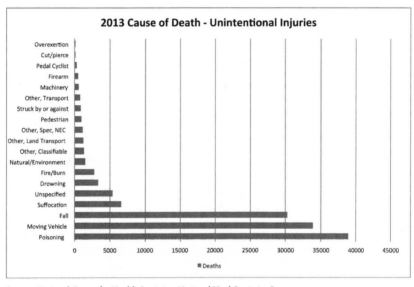

Source: National Center for Health Statistics, National Vital Statistics System

The gun community aims to make firearms owners even safer than they already are. One such effort targets youngsters, reducing safety to four simple steps, with a cadence and intent similar to "stop, drop, and roll."

The Eddie Eagle GunSafe® Program has as its mission to teach gun safety. According to its website:

> The program makes no value judgments about firearms, and no firearms are ever used in the program. Like swimming pools, electrical outlets, matchbooks and household poison, they're treated simply as a fact of everyday life. With firearms found in about half of all American households, it's a stance that makes sense.

When a child sees a gun, the four steps are: Stop. Don't touch. Run away. Tell a grown-up.

When my niece and nephew were young, I asked my sister for permission to talk to them about the program. Although she didn't own a gun, my sister couldn't be sure about her neighbors, and consented. Now adults, my niece and nephew never became gun owners; my safety talks did not somehow indoctrinate them to want guns. However, both are safer for having learned the basics years ago, and can still recite the steps today.

Astronaut Mark Kelly, the husband of Gabriella Giffords, tweeted in April 2015, "I don't agree w/ the @NRA on some big issues, but they deserve a lot of credit for teaching kids about gun safety. Eddieeagle.com." Recall that former Congresswoman Gabriella Giffords was herself a victim of gun violence, after which she and Mark became outspoken gun control advocates.

It's possible to be for gun control *and* be in favor of teaching gun safety.

Remove the Bubble Wrap

In our dangerous world, what is a parent's role? Is it to ban all the hazards, or is it to teach our children prudence?

Cam Edwards, host of NRA News' *Cam and Company* and The Blaze Radio Network's *40 Acres and a Fool* podcast, and author of the fatherhood guide *Heavy Lifting*, suggests that building their resilience is the proper way to prepare children for success.

"When we were kids, the world was dangerous, and it was also dangerous in the previous generations," said Edwards. "But we don't do our kids any favors by trying to remove all the potentially dangerous things from their lives. They never learn any coping skills, they never learn to tolerate others who are different, and they never really learn right from wrong."

Instead of treating them like "precious little snowflakes," damaged by the slightest adversity, he recommends admitting "that there are things in the world that might harm your kids. Admit that you will never know what all those things are. Admit that even if banning all those things were possible, it would never eliminate all the threats. Then teach your children how to be safe in a world that might harm them."

His advice is as true for neighbors seeking to live together in a civilized society as it is for parents.

CHAPTER 9

SCHOOLS THAT WORK

"Think of the children."

For many issues, even Fireworks issues, this sentiment inflames rather than illuminates. It's too often an emotional appeal instead of a reasoned one. But not with schools. With schools, "think of the children" is the only reasonable way to frame the issue.

It's no wonder parents question whether their child's school is going to provide what she needs for her future.

In the most recent international tests among 34 industrialized countries, 15-year-old Americans ranked 27th in math and 17th in reading. Colleges complain that too many of their freshmen require a remedial course. Businesses can't find enough skilled workers.

The U.S. Department of Education says its mission is "to promote student achievement and preparation for global competitiveness by fostering educational excellence and ensuring equal access." Since their inception in 1980 they have spent over $1.5 trillion in that cause. Yet schools have not gotten better, and many parents question the federal government's commitment to educational excellence.

In years past, "school choice" meant selecting which of the traditional neighborhood public schools a student should attend, in the rare case when a choice existed at all.

That's changed. Now, school choices include different public schools in a "choice district," secular private schools, religious private schools, charter schools in or out of one's home district, online schools, homeschooling, and more. With charter schools in all but eight states (as of January 2016) millions of families in America face decisions their parents never considered.

With all the choices now available, who is best suited to choose among them?

Who Knows Best?

The national divide is over whether professional government administrators or parents know best. It's another control versus choice dichotomy—between having professionals control education delivery and giving parents choice in their children's schools.

More of the Same

Those who think professionals know best generally favor traditional public schools. They prefer a centralized model of decision-making, relying on administrative experience to design the best programs for the most students. Their one-size-fits-all agenda supports a nationalized curriculum, standardized food programs for students, and uniform teacher pay, based on seniority and degree credentials rather than performance. Teachers unions generally support these positions, preferring to avoid the variances of merit pay and the competition between its members that such a system can create.

If a school is failing academically, those trusting professionals assume the school needs *more*: more teachers, more aides, more funding, and more textbooks. In their mind the centralized model is effective; it fails only when it has inadequate resources, which is why we see tax increase requests every election cycle across the country asking for more public school funds.

Those who think professionals know best typically oppose parental choice in education. They believe that parents are too provincial or shortsighted or biased or religious to make the choice that's in society's best interest. Instead of trusting parents, they trust public education professionals, such as the bureaucrats at the Department of Education, to know what is best for all of our children.

When these advocates "think of the children," they think of the inclusive, multicultural, empathetic, green, non-denominational, homogenous society that children educated their way will become.

My Tax Dollars, My Choice

Meatless Mondays. Prayer in public school. Dress codes. Textbook bias. Standardized testing. Sex-ed. These are only a few of the controversies in public schools, reflecting a nation and culture in flux. Likely, wherever you live, your tax dollars fund some element of public education that you don't support.

Consider new math versus traditional math. When I was a youngster, we memorized multiplication tables (our Pee-Chee folders provided a convenient table on the back for practice), used math flash cards, and solved for X. Math always had one answer. It was knowable and precise. Two plus two always equaled four.

Today, new math proponents ask, "If math were a color, what color would it be?" And, "How did Susie arrive at her answer that two plus two equals four?" If these questions from Everyday Math, a popular new math program, sound crazy to you, we are probably about the same age.

I prefer the former style of teaching over the new fuzzy approach to math. I prefer drills, while proponents of Everyday Math say those exercises stifle creativity. But however much I dislike Everyday Math, my tax dollars still pay for it in my district.

This mismatch between preference and payment extends to all areas of teaching, which means that taxpayers are not only paying for, but having their children taught with, methods, subject matter, and evaluations with which they disagree. Some of this is inevitable in any public education system, but unless we're trying to achieve *1984*'s Orwellian dystopia, a universal disparity of this order should not be our goal.

A Matter of Degree

Those who believe that professionals know best implicitly believe that parents don't. Maybe it's the advanced degrees prevalent among K-12 administrators and teachers, 52% of whom have a Master's Degree or higher. Among the general population, that number is 8.5%.

We wouldn't trust lawyers and doctors who don't have advanced degrees, they explain. Why should we trust our children's education—the future of our country—to anyone less trained?

Parents Know Best

Is having an advanced degree the only way to know the best educational options for students? Is it possible that parents, even those without a formal education, might know what's best for their own children?

Parents who think so see their children as theirs, rather than as wards of the government or of "the village" that it takes to raise a child. These parents recognize a personal moral obligation to see their own children educated.

The Right and Responsibility

Liberty Common High School, the top performing high school in Colorado, has as its universal principle of education:

> It is the right and responsibility of parents to direct the education and upbringing of their children.

Many parents agree. These parents, regardless of their education level, believe no one knows their children as well as they do. No one else has fed, clothed, housed, and loved them enough to choose an educational model that serves each child best.

One such parent is Bethany Drosendahl, a Colorado Springs mother and education advocate who describes herself as having a PhD in parenting. She considers herself lucky to have enjoyed the freedom to choose how to educate her children, and believes she has a moral obligation to ensure that those freedoms remain for future parents. Drosendahl accomplishes this by staying active in local and state educational issues as a parent advocate and by training other parents to exercise informed consent in their children's education.

"I am fortunate to live in a country where I have many choices," she says. "Traditional public school, public charter school, private school, home school. Maybe a little of each? Maybe something different for each child based on what is needed? In our school, there are four fourth-grade classes. Each teacher has a different style of instruction. For each of my three children I would select a different teacher. One teacher or style is not better or worse. They are simply different—which is great because so are my children."

Drosendahl is especially concerned about adopting one standardized curriculum and approach. "Just putting them all in the 'machine' and spitting out a uniform 'product.' Ugh! What that really looks like is a broken spirit. Each of us is a unique individual. I want that to be nurtured and honored. When students' learning environments are well matched to their learning styles, they like to learn!"

And Drosendahl is clear about who is best suited to ensure those unique environments, emphasizing the need for parents to actively participate at their children's schools. "The ultimate responsibility for demanding and ensuring the quality of local education lies in the hands of the individuals within that community, not the federal government," she said.

Administrators' advanced degrees do not absolve parents from the responsibility of planning their own children's education. Assuming that professional educators know better than parents ignores the truism that government ruins nearly everything it touches—and when that's our children, prudent vigilance ought to be our baseline.

My Dollars, My Choice

Any parent with multiple children knows that even given the same genetic pool and environment, siblings can vary considerably. This is one reason parents struggle with one-size-fits-all education. They instead appreciate the customized choices becoming more common across the country. Some schools specialize in math and science or performing arts or international studies or college preparation. Still others cater to special-needs students.

One of my neighbors has two daughters, Rachel and Beth, a year apart. Rachel is a talented artist and musician, who gets only average grades in math and science, but excels in and enjoys art, band, and choir. She has no interest in sports.

Beth loves math and the complexity of physics, but can't carry a tune and doesn't connect with the arts. Running on the cross-country team creates a solitude that clears her mind.

Despite growing up in the same household with the same parents, the two girls differ completely in their interests, approaches to learning, and aptitudes. For their parents, having school choice allows them to send each girl to a school that kindles her passions. Imagine if all communities respected diversity this much, and catered to the unique qualities that set each student apart by creating a plethora of school options.

Selecting among such schools is not some arcane, inscrutable process beyond the capacity of parents. As consumers, we're all accustomed to shopping for the products and services that best meet our needs, in things as important as health care, career choice, and where to live. It should be no different for the decisions that most shape our children's futures.

Public Options: Choice from Charters

Nominal school choice is meaningful only when there is a variety of schools from which to choose. Increasingly, those choices are becoming available, often via charter schools. Charters are free, public schools, publicly funded but run by parents or other private groups, and usually with a specific educational specialty.

More than 6800 public charter schools operate nationwide, enrolling more than 2.9 million students—about 6% of all public school attendees—and growing. In the 2015-2016 school year more than 400 charter schools opened, and 272 ceased operations. This dynamism reflects a community responding to the demands of its parents, opening more schools where needed and closing those that underperform or fail to serve. Because charter schools are part of the public school system, they foster competition in their associated districts, along with the innovation and accountability needed to thrive. Districts can also close traditional neighborhood schools that don't perform well enough to attract families, just like their charter counterparts, allocating resources to the best performing schools.

Not just public schools have changed. Private and religious schools have also expanded their accessibility, by implementing scholarship programs for children in the poorest and lowest-performing school districts. These privately funded programs create more options, especially for the most vulnerable populations.

How does America feel about this increasing array of educational choices? Attitudes now reflect a preference for local control and accountability, the two hallmarks of school choice. The Center for Education Reform's national 2013 poll found:

- 73% of respondents support charter schools.
- By a 56% to 15% margin, Americans prefer local school boards over the federal government.
- 62% favor performance pay for teachers.

These attitudes toward choice in education aren't following traditional left/right philosophies. Instead, they reveal an increasing distrust of government control of decisions and an increasing trust in individuals making their own educational choices.

What do those choices actually look like? Around the country, public charter schools are arising to meet a range of educational needs. As options like these become more widespread, imagine the appreciation of parents empowered to shop from a menu of schools that gives them truly meaningful selections.

Learning with Autism at Spectrum

Frustrated with the educational opportunities available for students with autism, a group of parents in North Salt Lake, Utah, formed Spectrum Academy in 2006. This public charter school now serves almost 1000 students on two campuses, specializing in teaching children on the autism spectrum. Acknowledging parents is central to Spectrum's philosophy. As the school tells its families: "As parents in the Spectrum Community, you are a valuable resource. You know your child better than anyone."

Founded by parents of children with Asperger's Syndrome and high-functioning autism, these parents wanted what every parent wants: for their children to be successful, happy adults. Opening originally as a K-8 school, Spectrum's elementary and secondary schools soon filled. In response to long waiting lists, the school opened a second campus and is expanding though grades 9-12.

Since the school specializes in autism, the teachers and staff—many of whom have autism in their own families—expect the unexpected. So how does Spectrum Academy look different from other schools? In a 2014 interview with *Deseret News*, Spectrum Academy's Director of Development Brad Nelson explained:

> "It will look like a typical classroom until you look more closely and see a kid sitting on a bouncy ball chair, or another child wearing earphones to help him focus on the teacher talking, or see another one with a small screen on his desk. There will be some kids fidgeting with toys under their desks, which are allowed, for their specialized sensory needs.
>
> "It takes them out of a resource class at a typical school and puts them in a more conducive and comfortable environment that is right for

them," Nelson said, adding that with autism being largely a social disorder, many students who suffer the condition can't function normally in a typical classroom.

Spectrum's accommodations are anything but typical, which is exactly what its families and students need.

Focusing on Dyslexia at MAX Charter

MAX Charter School, a public charter school since 2007 in the bayou city of Thibodaux, was Louisiana's first school to focus on students with dyslexia. It is designed for students in first through eighth grade who struggle with dyslexia and related learning differences. The school's name honors Maxine Giardina, a pioneer in dyslexia recognition.

People with dyslexia have a particularly hard time understanding the structure of words, but the kinds of compensating strategies used at MAX prepare the students to hold their own academically when they transition to secondary education. Master teacher Rebecca Walker sees that progress firsthand. "They've been in classrooms where the majority is moving on and getting it and they're not. That beats down a kid," she said. "They come to me not knowing the names of letters. By the end of the year they're reading. It's amazing to see that progress. I see it across the board, the whole child. They're growing academically and socially."

For the 110 students at MAX, that growth is directly related to the existence of a school customized to address their specific needs.

Teaching STEM at Tesla

While some schools gear their methods towards certain types of learners, others emphasize certain topics and career choices. Tesla Engineering Charter School, in Appleton, Wisconsin, serves students interested in science, technology, engineering, and math (STEM). Founded in 2002, this public charter school recognizes that its students thrive by designing, building, playing with, and breaking things.

With courses like Engineering Design, Digital Electronics, and Computer Integrated Manufacturing—and none in music or dance—Tesla lives its mission to prepare those with aptitude and passion to pursue STEM careers. And its philosophy reflects the broader school choice conversation: "There's more than one path to travel, and not all paths lead to the same destination." The families at Tesla appreciate the engineering path the school encourages students to follow.

Self-Pacing at Carpe Diem

Carpe Diem Learning Schools, tuition-free public charter schools with campuses in four states, has developed its own education system—a blended learning model that combines online learning with face-to-face instruction. Carpe Diem's blended learning style allows students to move at their own pace through their computerized lessons, and supplements that with additional support through workshops, one-on-one interaction with teachers, and student learning groups. Students sit at individual cubicles, for example, instead of in group classrooms.

Students advance at their own rate in individual subjects, without changing grades. This also means that students below grade level in one subject have the opportunity to catch up without the worry of being held back a grade. This self-pacing is the ultimate in individualized learning: it's likely that no two students ever share the same exact daily lessons. Because of the flexibility in pacing, students also learn how to be more self-directed, in preparation for college and their future careers.

Despite the use of online instruction, students at Carpe Diem receive considerable personal attention. The teachers in the core knowledge areas of curriculum remain with the students through all six years of instruction. A math teacher who learns about a seventh-grader's strengths and weaknesses, for example, stays with that student through graduation.

How does all of this translate into results? At the Yuma Arizona campus, the first Carpe Diem school, the results have been striking:

- Leading the county for four straight years on the Arizona Instrument for Measuring Standards (AIMS) test
- Leading the state in student growth for two consecutive years
- Earning a rating of 10 of 10 by parents and Great Schools.com
- Averaging two years of curriculum completion for every year a student is in school

Although its aggregate results are strong, Carpe Diem is not for everyone. Those students uncomfortable taking some responsibility for their education or who aren't dedicated will do poorly, and might leave the school.

As they should, in a marketplace of true educational choices.

Choices, Choices

With the continued increase in charter school options, these choices will only expand, helping students capitalize on their own interests and unique capabilities. Parents, challenged by having children with unique learning styles, might find schools that deliver exactly what their children individually need. These experiments in customized education also benefit taxpayers, who want their education funds spent efficiently, at schools that can best serve specific populations.

But in a robust marketplace of educational choices, public charters aren't the only option for those looking beyond their traditional neighborhood public schools.

Private Options: Not Only for the Wealthy

There was a time when private schools were only for wealthy families. Elite private schools provided advanced curricula, a college preparatory focus, and the contacts and networks necessary to give students a leg up in college. But they barred their doors to the poor.

Not anymore.

HOPE Christian High School

In inner city Milwaukee, surrounded by some of the worst performing schools in the country, lies HOPE Christian High School, where for the last four years 100% of its seniors have been accepted to college. As a whole, only 60% of high school seniors in Milwaukee even graduate high school.

Nearly all of HOPE's students qualify for free or reduced lunch, a majority come from single-parent homes, and most attend through Milwaukee's Parental Choice Program, which provides qualifying families with a state voucher to supplement private school tuition. Income is no barrier to attendance.

HOPE challenges its students to defy the community's legacy of underperformance. They adhere to a strict dress code and are held to demanding academic standards. Teachers, recognizing that circumstances outside of school have often held their students back in the past, provide them with their cell phone numbers for off-hours help, 24 hours a day.

Jamie Luehring, HOPE's executive director, dismisses the notion that poverty excuses academic failure. "Anyone who says that kids can't learn because of their circumstances has never seen the power of a high performing school subscribed to the belief that not only can all kids learn, but they simply will learn."

Arrupe Jesuit

Arrupe Jesuit High School in North Denver is part of a network of 47 private, college-preparatory Jesuit high schools across the country. The network's Denver campus serves low-income, minority students, most of whom enter the school several grades behind their peers. Yet, despite their disadvantaged start, all of Arrupe Jesuit's 2015 graduating class were accepted to the college of their choice. Roughly half of these students were the first in their family to graduate high school; 92% were the first in their families to attend college.

The average family income at the Denver campus is only $31,000 per year—60% of the national median. This income cannot support private school tuition, but Arrupe Jesuit has made it possible. With its Corporate Work Study Program, Arrupe cooperates with area partner companies where students earn valuable work experience and are able to fund a portion of their own tuition.

To accommodate both work and school commitments, Arrupe Jesuit uses a longer school day and year. Parents pay a small portion of the tuition, which may be as little as $100 per month. Supplemental scholarships provide the remainder.

Arrupe Jesuit has never turned a student away for lack of ability to pay.

Low-achieving, traditional schools may be a barrier to achievement, but it's a myth that poverty is the reason. In Denver, Arrupe Jesuit proves that family income is irrelevant. When parents take an active role, students are held to high standards, and a community invests in its own future, then the benefits of a high-performing private school are available to anyone.

Private Tuition Scholarships

Although private schools sponsor most financial aid themselves, numerous scholarship programs help pay for private school tuition, and most accept only low-income children. Children's Scholarship Fund, for example, provides scholarships for more than 24,000 students nationwide. As is common with such programs, Children's Scholarship Fund requires its recipient families to pay at least 25% of their tuition each year, making them fully invested in their children's education.

No government requirement forces these scholarship organizations to focus on low-income children. They instead, voluntarily, choose to help low-income families. Without government prodding, without intrusive mandates, and without external criteria, communities help their own most disadvantaged children.

What's Fair?

Rich families have always been able to send their children to the most expensive private schools, or to put a bow on a BMW for a daughter's 16th birthday. Is that fair to all the middle-class families?

And yet those paying for private school do so twice: once in their child's tuition and again in their property tax bill. Is that fair?

Perhaps fairness ought to start with thinking about the children. What if the amount of tax money that pays for one child's education were assigned to that specific child? He could get a certificate with his own name on it, to be used for the school that best fits him. Parents, the ones who know their children best, would use their own judgment to find that match, and the result would be a very individualized approach to education.

The system would be more fair for the richer families, whose double-taxation is punitive on the surface. And it would be fairer for the poorer students, who would have the opportunity to attend previously unattainable private schools. Milwaukee's HOPE Christian succeeds because of this model. Although Milwaukee's vouchers provide only 40% of per-pupil spending (public schools there receive $14,863 per student annually; Milwaukee's vouchers are $6,442), that's coincidentally the annual tuition at HOPE.

There's a side benefit, one the marketplace always reveals when consumers are empowered with means and choice. Once schools begin to compete for the children, and for the certificates, the schools overall will improve. Competition rewards effectiveness, and where would we want that more than in our educational system?

Anti-Political Solutions

Government ruins nearly everything, and education is no exception. Compared to their international counterparts, American students are sub-par. They often aren't ready for college level courses, and the Department of Education wastes billions every year. If the status quo—expecting that government is best able to improve education—isn't working, what will?

Enable a Marketplace

Imagine shopping for your child's education just like you'd shop for a new laptop or house. Tools are increasingly available to allow exactly that. But instead of starting the process by reading reviews on *Consumer Reports* or Zillow.com, you'd instead explore GreatSchools.org or your state's accountability data. The Colorado Department of Education, for example, provides a series of dashboards called SchoolView that compare performance, enrollment, safety, and more in every public school across the state.

You might follow your initial search for a laptop or a house by asking your friends about their computers or communities. You might visit your local retailer to explore a laptop hands-on, or walk a neighborhood to feel its character.

We are all accustomed to shopping this way for most consumer products, and making informed choices that reflect our own research. How would we respond if we were forced to accept the taxpayer-funded laptop that our state government determined was best for us? One model; no choices. This is the computer we've chosen for you. This is the house we've decided suits you best. Take it or leave it. And you can't leave it.

Public funding of education is widely viewed as a proper use of our tax dollars, but a monopoly on the public delivery of that education is not at all a universal good.

Roll Back Common Core

A thriving and diverse educational marketplace recognizes that all students are not the same, don't have the same interests, and learn in different ways. Local governing boards and neighborhood schools of all types are close enough to their communities to recognize these differences in ways federal bureaucracies never can.

Which is why parents are resisting Common Core State Standards nationwide.

This set of national education standards and testing for K–12 arose from the National Governors Association's attempt in 2009 to create a common definition of success for students across America. Within months, 42 states adopted the standards. Coincidentally, that adoption increased a state's chances to receive federal Race to the Top grants, a $4.3 billion pool of funds allocated under The Recovery Act—the American Recovery and Reinvestment Act of 2009. Incentives matter, and states desperate for funds chased the money.

Those funds are now gone. Coincidentally, three states have now repealed their adoption of Common Core, and many more are considering it.

It was not only for money that states adopted the Common Core standards and are now abandoning them, but the allure of federal dollars too often skews local politicians' objectivity. Like gold cannonballs shot from beyond a wall of good intentions, the insidious influence of money from afar is one way that government consistently ruins nearly everything.

The standards were meant to codify and measure what students ought to know, but one national standard for all children does not respect local environments or students' individuality. Even teachers see this. Six in ten say they are "worried or frustrated" with the new Common Core State Standards. When the government enforces solutions and uses its clout to "fix" problems, states are whipsawed by the caprice, and their residents suffer from the instability.

It's unreasonable to expect that the federal Department of Education in Washington, D.C. knows best what each child needs. But even if the ultimate educational responsibility does not devolve all the way to individual households—most parents aren't suited to be home-school teachers—at least the function should be as local as possible. At a minimum, states should operate as 50 laboratories for innovation, and choose standards and curricula that best serve their own residents.

Spread What Works

Charter schools work. Not every one, of course—which is one of their advantages. Those that fail to serve fail to stay open, keeping resources allocated where they do the most good. But across the country charters are among many states' best performing schools.

Although charter high schools make up only 6% of public high schools nationwide, they outperform traditional public schools, as these 2014 lists show:

- *U.S. News and World Report* ranking of best high schools: 24 out of the 100 schools were charters
- *Washington Post* high school Challenge Index: 31 out of the top 100 schools were charters
- *Newsweek* list of America's Best High Schools: 17 out of the 100 schools were charters
- *Newsweek* "25 Schools doing the Most with the Least" list: 10 out of the 25 schools were charters

Critics suggest that these results ensue because charters self-select for traditionally high-performing populations, but according to Stanford University's Center for Research on Education Outcomes:

> Importantly, charters are producing large academic gains for the most historically disadvantaged students, notably low-income Hispanic and African American students, and English language learners.

And yet despite their demonstrated success, charters are not yet allowed in eight states.

Grassroots efforts propelled charter school legislation across the country, but some states remain without charter schools, or with weak authorizing laws, or mired in politically unfriendly environments.

Parents in those locales need direct political action to achieve what the rest of the country already enjoys. The goal is attainable: parents have spearheaded such efforts for the last 20 years. Perhaps in another 20, that much parent activism will no longer be necessary.

2015 Number of Charter Schools by State					
State	# Schools	State	# Schools	State	# Schools
CA	1234	UT	111	NH	26
TX	723	TN	100	CT	24
FL	656	NM	99	KS	10
AZ	535	IN	91	VA	9
OH	373	NJ	89	ME	7
MI	300	MA	81	WA	7
NY	257	MO	68	WY	4
WI	244	SC	68	IA	3
CO	226	AR	50	MS	2
PA	175	MD	50	AL	0
MN	165	ID	48	KY	0
NC	161	NV	38	MT	0
IL	145	OK	35	ND	0
LA	143	HI	34	NE	0
OR	127	AK	28	SD	0
DC	115	RI	28	VT	0
GA	115	DE	27	WV	0

Source: PublicCharter.org New and Closed Report, Feb. 2015

Fund Schools Equitably

Allowing charter schools is only the first step. Securing fair funding is what makes them viable and lasting. As public schools, charters receive public funds; they just don't get the same funding that their traditional counterparts do.

Charters generally get an equitable share of per-pupil revenue (PPR)—the amount that each state allocates annually for every K-12 student. But what they don't get is funding for facilities, the second biggest item in any school's budget, after personnel costs.

Traditional school facilities are funded outside of the PPR model, using bonds, mill levies, and property tax increases to secure the actual property and facilities. Charters are almost never included in these extra sources of funding. And although some states allocate a nominal facilities supplement to PPR, the amounts are an order of magnitude below actual facilities costs.

The net, including accounting for facilities, is that charter schools receive only 64% of their non-charter counterparts' funding. Which means that charters, almost without exception, must use per-pupil money to bolster inadequate facilities budgets. But every dollar spent on keeping a roof overhead is one less to pay teachers or tutor students or buy books.

Lawmakers should rectify this unfair treatment by providing public charter schools equal access to the funding available to traditional public schools. Continually asking charters to "do more with less" is a disservice to the 6% of students who attend them.

Issue Vouchers Without Strings

The ultimate practical expression of favoring private choice over public control is to retain public funding of education, but remove its exclusive public delivery. That is, have the money follow the child to his or her school of choice, whether that school is a public or private one.

Via voucher, certificate, or opportunity scholarship, the result is to return to parents the responsibility for the quality of their children's education. This is the most direct way to ensure that parents get the specific education they've already paid for, and to get the choice of school that best serves their children.

Shouldn't all students have the chance to learn in ways that foster their full potential? Shouldn't students who need extra courses in math, science, and physics be able to attend a STEM-specialized school, even when tuition is a barrier?

Private schools are the right answer for many, because they can exist only when they offer a type of school their community wants. Some will teach to certain special needs; others might focus on competitive sports, performing arts, trade-school partnerships, or college preparation. They might be religious. In fact, most are: 80% of private-school students attend religious private schools. True parental choice acknowledges this, and allows parents to choose the secular or religious school they deem best.

Already 13 states and the District of Columbia offer vouchers in some form, but usually with qualifications. Vouchers might be available only to students from failing schools, having certain disabilities, being below a certain income, or living in foster care. These qualifications are recognition that all schools can't best support all students, that one size does not fit all. Vouchers in those cases support the most vulnerable students.

But all students are vulnerable.

All students—poor, different, brilliant, talented, homeless, struggling, or excelling—are vulnerable when sent to schools not suited for them.

We would never tolerate forced choices in any other product when the consumer needs are so diverse. There is no one car or shoe or deodorant for everyone. Neither is there one type of school for everyone, but without vouchers it's as if there are no choices for many families.

Where vouchers exist now, they come with strings attached. Those qualifications prevent enough parents from exercising the freedom of choice that could empower an effective public and private marketplace. We should cut the strings. Vouchers, certificates, or opportunity scholarships should require that recipient schools have appropriate accreditation. Other than that, the government should leave to parents all decisions about where tuition is spent.

Repeal Blaine Amendments

But doesn't this mean that public funds will directly support religious institutions? Even religions with which you might disagree?

No.

The money is being handed back to the parents, where it came from, and the parents are choosing what is best for their children. The public coffers should be blind to its delivery, as long as the chosen school meets state-mandated sanctioning requirements.

The difference is not just semantic. It's a meaningful distinction about choice versus control. Frame the issue instead as if the government said, "Please take care of your child's education. It's important enough that we're publicly funding it, but use this money only at a government store, and avoid all religious contamination."

Now substitute "health care" or "clothing" or "nutrition" or "community service" or "morals" or "soul" for "education."

Unthinkable.

Nonetheless, many states are currently prevented from giving their parents these options. The barrier is something called the Blaine Amendment.

In 1875 America was a predominantly Protestant country, facing increasing immigration from Catholics. Arriving Catholics wanted their prayers recited in schools, while locals preferred that prayers remain exclusively Protestant. Acting on their beliefs, Catholic parents began to create and send their children to Catholic schools—public ones.

Yet anti-Catholic sentiment was strong, and voters pressured lawmakers to prevent tax money from funding these new Catholic schools. Spearheading this effort nationally, Congressman James G. Blaine proposed an amendment to the U.S. Constitution. It read:

> No State shall make any law respecting an establishment of religion, or prohibiting the free exercise thereof; and no money raised by taxation in any State for the support of public schools, or derived from any public fund therefore, nor any public lands devoted thereto, shall ever be under the control of any religious sect; nor shall any money so raised or lands so devoted be divided between religious sects or denominations.

This passed overwhelmingly in the House of Representatives, but failed by four votes in the Senate. Nonetheless, in its wake 36 states adopted their own constitutional amendments restricting tax dollars from funding religious institutions. Those today are collectively known as Blaine amendments, and are the primary legal impediment to vouchers nationwide.

Even those in favor of these amendments, those who prefer to maintain a strict division between church and state, need to consider the cost. Blaine amendments disempower parents. And if parents hold ultimate responsibility for their children's education, then eliminating religious private schools from their choices skews the market too strongly in favor of government-only options. Instead of relying on antiquated laws rooted in bigotry, we should let each family choose for itself whether a private school is the right choice, and whether that school should be religious or secular.

To serve all of our students best we should worry less about separating church and state, and instead concentrate on separating school and state.

CHAPTER 10

Strong Marriages

Marriage is a deeply personal choice.

Today, at least. In the United States.

Within some cultural pockets parents arrange the marriages of their children, but we generally choose our spouses ourselves. We're accustomed to independence in such important decisions, and few decisions can have as long-lasting an impact as choosing a marriage partner.

But excessive government intrusion has turned marriage into a political stand-in for traditional values and coerced association, making it a playpen for moralistic and anti-capitalist mischief, and interfering with choices that ought to remain ours alone.

As enforcers of marriage contracts—a necessary and appropriate role—government presumes to also have authority over who can be married, who can authorize the licensing, who can conduct the ceremony, who must do business with the betrothed couple, and who must subsidize the arrangement.

So much public policy for such a deeply personal choice.

A Legacy of Restrictions

Fundamentally, marriage is a contract governing cohabitation, the birthright of children, allocation of certain benefits, and the disposition of property. As the sole enforcer of contracts, government must adjudicate if one party violates the terms.

But for much of history, government has intervened in the selection process as well.

Chattel Can't Choose

Early marriage was anything but a deeply personal choice. For centuries, churches and parents used marriage to cement relationships between families, keep bloodlines intact, and manage property transfer. Women were assets, traded along with money, livestock, and other household goods.

Early marriage had no government marriage license, no government approval, and no government rules. Those conventions came from families and churches—conventions such as the father walking his daughter down the aisle to "give her away." That tradition echoes a transfer of the bride, once viewed as chattel property (from the same linguistic root as "cattle"), from the father to the new husband.

Today's sweet tradition now makes us dab tears from our eyes, but in early marriage this was a business transaction. The bride may never have met the groom before the wedding.

And it didn't matter. Not to property.

Whom You May and May Not Marry

Families weren't the only institutions removing choice from the marriage equation. Governments did also, and with equally dehumanizing restrictions. Early American states chose to start controlling marriages only when they were trying to control *interracial* marriages. American colonial governments "protected" their white citizens from consorting with black or brown or red or yellow people. Laws against interracial marriage and relationships were on the books in most U.S. states until the 1950s and 1960s.

Not until 1967, in *Loving v. Virginia*, did the U.S. Supreme Court finally declare the remaining state laws against interracial marriage unconstitutional. The ruling overturned miscegenation laws still on the books in 16 states, laws that for most of our country's history had barred consenting adults from associating as they wished.

In its 1967 decision, the court declared:

> The Fourteenth Amendment requires that the freedom of choice to marry not be restricted by invidious *racial* discriminations. Under our Constitution, the freedom to marry, or not to marry, a person *of another race* resides with the individual and cannot be infringed by the State.

The italics are mine. I prefer imagining the broader acceptance that would result if even those italicized qualifiers were removed from Chief Justice Warren's comments, so that discrimination of any kind not be allowed.

What God Has Joined Together

The power to choose a marriage partner is amplified when it's accompanied by full choice in dissolving that marriage, a choice restricted by law for decades.

Leave It To Beaver, the iconic TV mainstay from the late 1950s and early 1960s, showed us the idyllic nuclear family. Ward Cleaver never came home angry from a tough day, and he never worked overtime. Homemaker June Cleaver was coiffed and made-up, with the dinner table already set when the breadwinner got home from work. And despite their boyhood antics, sons Wally and Beaver were both good boys who never got in to any *real* trouble.

Certainly when *Leave It To Beaver* aired it *was* a simpler time. The TV series, however, was only entertainment—not reality. Marriages of that time, and of the decades to follow, were not as idyllic as the Cleaver household, but a lack of choices hid much of the reality. Notwithstanding June Cleaver being content to care for a husband and children, women of that generation had few choices. Marriage was the default option for a young woman in the 1950s and 1960s, especially considering the job market: many companies wouldn't hire women if men were available, nor were wages equitable when jobs were available. The notion of "women's work" tainted the marketplace and cemented the division of labor at home, creating an ongoing and oppressive trap.

Until no-fault divorce. Although the divorce rate was flat in the '50s and early '60s, "no-fault divorce" laws came into effect in the late '60s and early '70s. Women, many of them stuck in unhappy marriages, finally had a direct escape without the legal fiction of showing wrongdoing that had become commonplace.

Depending on whom you ask, women were either happier then (because they were fulfilling societal expectations and didn't have so many disparate pressures) or they are happier now (because they have more choices). In either case, the same government that only reluctantly introduced choice into the marriage process also only reluctantly gave up the authority to justify dissolving those bonds.

The real questions for then and now are: Who should choose which people can marry each other, and who should choose when they can divorce?

The Times They Are a-Changin'

Despite a legacy of restrictions, marriages and families today are more diverse than ever.

No Single Definition

As a proxy for the broader concept of voluntary association, marriage and family structures vary worldwide, just as cultures do. Polygamy—any group marriage—is found in more than 1000 societies across the globe. Among those, polygyny (multiple wives) is much more common than polyandry (multiple husbands). Different cultures reflect different customs of association—some for practical reasons and some for traditional ones.

Polygyny is found in parts of Asia, Africa, and the Middle East. Histories of warfare there often created demographic mismatches: almost every dead fighter was one fewer potential husband. And yet in poor societies a woman might need a husband to survive, even if it meant sharing one. But even where polygyny is permitted, only a small percentage of men practice it. It seems a universal rule that having multiple wives is expensive.

A handful of smaller, matriarchal societies exist as well, including the Mosuo in China and the Indonesian Minangkabau. In each, women rule, household arrangements are communal, and, to westerners' eyes, the "father's" role could best be described as vague.

Nuclear Counter-Reaction

But we don't have to look across the world to find family structures unlike June and Ward Cleaver's. In the United States, blended families of all varieties now account for 40% of households. The nuclear family is no longer the norm even here.

Nor is marriage a preference for an increasing number of millennials. A 2014 Pew Research poll concluded that 25% of them will never get married. Attitudes have evolved about living together and having children outside of marriage. Disparaging terms like "living in sin" and "illegitimate child" have given way to more benign phrases like "shacking up," "cohabitating," and "baby mama."

Decades ago, most women needed a husband for financial security. Today, 40% of women are either the sole or primary wage earners for their families. Nearly 2 million men are stay-at-home dads, a number that has doubled in the last 25 years.

Decades ago, interracial and interfaith marriages were a social taboo. Now, more than 8% of marriages are interracial, and 40% are interfaith. More couples are deciding not to have children at all, and some fertile couples are choosing to adopt.

Choices that would have sounded peculiar in decades past are now commonplace. Imagine the reaction of the *Leave It to Beaver* generation if they knew what was coming.

With voluntary family associations so diverse, can it be the proper role of government to regulate and reward one specific configuration?

Inevitable As the Demographic Tide

In June 2015, the U.S. Supreme Court ruled 5-to-4 that Americans are guaranteed the right to same-sex marriage. By the time of the ruling 35 states had already sanctioned it, with more pending. At that rate, it was all but inevitable that same-sex marriage soon would have been legal nationwide even without the highest court's ruling.

The change in attitude was swift, in cultural terms. As recently as 1996, President Clinton signed the Defense of Marriage Act, banning the federal government from recognizing same-sex marriages. As a presidential candidate in 2008, Senator Barack Obama told Pastor Rick Warren that he believed marriage was between one man and one woman.

In the past 18 years, U.S. support for same-sex marriage has increased 28%, with a majority now supporting its legality. In that same span, even Republican support rose 14%. And the numbers are more startling among millennials. A full 70% of those born after 1981 support same-sex marriage. Young people continue to be the biggest supporters of same-sex marriage, including 61% of Republicans under age 30.

Given the dramatic differences in support by age, it's clear that demography was destiny. With or without the Supreme Court's actions,

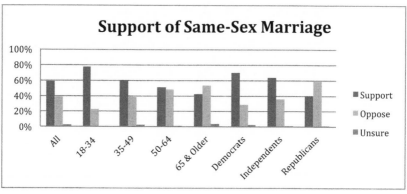

Source: CNN/ORC Poll, 2015

tomorrow's Americans were certain to legalize same-sex marriage over time.

Now that same-sex marriage is law, its supporters and detractors each may imagine that on this topic there is still work to do.

The Plural of Spouse Is Spice

Proponents of one-man-one-woman marriage invoke a slippery slope argument: "If we allowed *this* kind of marriage, then what's next? *That* kind of marriage?"

Perhaps *that* kind of marriage ought to be next, given the trajectory of history. So far in America we've progressed to voluntary marriage, interfaith marriage, interracial marriage, and now same-sex marriage. Decide for yourself if there's some place along that path where inclusiveness and voluntary association should matter less than government rule. I don't see one.

Alarmists worry about what's next on this slippery slope. "Next comes polygamy, then incest, then children, then animals, then inanimate objects!" they fret. "Where does it stop?"

For me, it stops at consenting adult humans. Which, it turns out, isn't such a slippery slope after all.

Does this mean we will turn into a nation of polygamists? Personally, I don't know anyone who has the time to be attentive to one spouse, much less two or more. But how is it my business, or the government's, to tell people with whom and how to associate?

Not that the government doesn't try.

Freedom from Association

A dangerous backlash is emerging as same-sex marriage is legalized across the country: the trend of lawsuits to force providers of wedding services (florists, bakers, photographers, etc.) to serve a same-sex wedding, even when the proprietors object to such ceremonies. There is even a move to require pastors of churches that oppose same-sex marriage to officiate at those weddings. Compulsion of this sort, forcing action directly against one's beliefs, can't be a part of a free society.

More Than Just a Cake

A notable landmark case concerns Masterpiece Cakeshop in Denver. Owner Jack Phillips, a lifelong Christian, never hid his opposition to same-sex marriage, considering it a direct violation of his religion. So when in 2012 a same-sex couple asked him to design a custom wedding cake, he declined, considering it sacrilege to use his artistic expression to celebrate a ceremony that his faith opposed.

The couple expected this refusal. It was their whole reason for choosing Masterpiece Cakeshop specifically, and the first step in bringing a discrimination suit, which they won, while crying crocodile tears:

> Being denied service by Masterpiece Cakeshop was offensive and dehumanizing especially in the midst of arranging what should be a joyful family celebration. No one should fear being turned away from a public business because of who they are.

But they weren't turned away. Phillips was happy to sell any item off his shelf to this couple or any other customer—gay, straight, or anything in between. "I don't make cakes for same-sex weddings," he told them, "but I'll make you birthday cakes, shower cakes, or sell you cookies and brownies." He refused to make an individualized cake not because of who they were, but because of what the cake represented. He declined to use his creative talents to convey a message he opposed, for the same reason that he refused to make cakes celebrating Halloween, racism, or anti-American themes.

Dozens of Denver bakeries would have been happy to make a custom creation for the couple, but the plaintiffs weren't shopping for cake; they were shopping for headlines.

In microcosm, the incident illustrates a fundamental question in a free society: Do we have the right to decide for ourselves which goods we must make, which messages we must say, and which customers we must serve?

When Protected Class Meets Classless Behavior

Marriage is about free association. Why not allow the commerce surrounding it the same liberty?

It is currently illegal to refuse to do business with someone based on a wide variety of classifications. The Civil Rights Act of 1964 and The Americans with Disabilities Act of 1990 mandate that "public accommodations"—retail stores, rental establishments, schools, and more—must not discriminate based on race, color, religion, or national origin. Many states add sexual orientation, age, and gender to the list.

Is that proper in a free country?

If a business chose not to allow people of a certain race to shop at its store, that would be morally reprehensible.

But should the government weigh in? Is the force of government the only remedy for such behavior? What would the free market do differently than government to address such behavior?

What would consumers do once it became known that a local business—let's say a bookstore—said that anyone of Asian ancestry was no longer allowed to shop there? Imagine the uproar in the community! Pickets and demonstrations would be only the beginning. News media would descend in a frenzy to interview outraged protesters and excoriate the owners, who would hide under their jackets as they pressed through the angry throng. Sales would plummet as the news, social media, and online review sites expressed outrage. Customers would avoid the bookstore and tell their friends to do the same, and the owners and employees would face widespread scorn. Workers would resign in protest. The bookstore would soon go out of business.

But all those actions would be voluntary: the business excluding certain customers, others expressing indignation, viral news coverage, a *de facto* boycott, resignations, condemnations, closure. All without government.

This example is extreme, but in anticipation of it even a racist shop owner would never enact such a policy. Business success forbids it. A government prohibition on top of that is not only superfluous, it's expensive and condescending, needing layers of regulations and inspectors and lawyers and nannies to enforce what civilized citizens could do better without government's paternalism and scolding.

Apply this same logic and process to Masterpiece Cakeshop. Some would find its refusal to make custom cakes for same-sex marriages to be hateful, and decide not to shop there. They might spread the word to a like-minded community, raising a public outcry and censure. New customers might choose to frequent the bakery for exactly the opposite reason. Other local bakeries would reach out, happy to serve Masterpiece's prior clientele.

On balance, the marketplace would decide whether a policy based on voluntary association would lead to business success or failure. Actions have consequences, and not only because of government policy, but because of more efficient, uncoerced private choices. I trust my friends, neighbors, and the voluntary free market to solve a problem like this more than I trust the government to solve it.

As of 2016, Masterpiece Cakeshop no longer sells wedding cakes— not to customers of any sexual identity. When we let the government intervene in private commerce like this, both the community and the store owner are poorer as a result.

The Friendship Nine Was of Its Time

How is this different from the Friendship Nine being refused service at McCrory's segregated lunch counter in Rock Hill, South Carolina in 1961? Shouldn't the law have forced those customers to be served?

Recall that the sit-ins in the '60s were protests of the segregation laws. As strange as it sounds today, the law of the land required black and white customers to sit separately, eat separately and, in many cases, shop separately. This state-sponsored segregation was codified in 1896, when, in *Plessy v. Ferguson*, the Supreme Court endorsed a misguided "separate but equal" race structure—cementing in place Jim Crow laws for more than another half a century.

Though "separate but equal" was struck down in the landmark 1954 *Brown v. Board of Education* decision, its odious legacy remained. Groups like the Friendship Nine used civil disobedience to erase its last vestiges. Acts of this kind, and a burgeoning enlightenment across the country, led to the necessary 1964 Civil Rights Act. In a time without an empowered citizenry, only the force of government could effect the kind of nationwide change needed to jolt America into race consciousness.

That was then. This is now.

Now everyone has a cell phone, so everyone is a news reporter, a restaurant reviewer, an activist, a videographer. Everyone is one viral meme away from national headlines and from summoning civil rights activists on the next plane to town.

We all have power—of the media and of the pocketbook.

In the segregated south of 1964, black customers didn't have a choice. Today, we are free to buy from businesses we like, shun those we don't, and watch the marketplace shift in response. Necessary as it was then, the forcing hand of government is no longer needed to make people do business with each other.

But it still does.

Freedom from Speech

In the face of laws demanding that he use his creative talents to support a cause he opposed, baker Jack Phillips tried to carve out a religious exemption, using his faith as his only justification to do as he wished with his own business.

In my opinion, his argument was too narrow. A religious exemption is incomplete and plays favorites. Business owners should have the discretion to not do business with those who offend any of their values— not just the religious ones.

Following the reasoning of the decision against Phillips, a gay T-shirt maker can be forced to print "God Hates Fags" T-shirts for the Westboro Baptist Church. A black tattoo artist has to ink a skinhead's confederate flag. A Jewish printer must create business cards for the KKK. An American videographer can be compelled to film a jihadist "Death to America" video.

The list of loathsome coercions is endless.

This precedent is beyond dangerous to any notion of freedom. Within the principle of freedom of speech is the freedom from compulsion of speech. The freedom to say what you want must include the freedom to not say what you don't want, or it's no freedom at all. And speech need not be words; it can be symbols as iconic as flags or wedding cakes. Courts have found items as disparate as painting, sculptures, nude dancing, and tattoos to constitute speech. As "artistic expression" they even earn an additional legal protection to not be compelled, even in the face of the otherwise obligatory public accommodation that the 1964 Civil Rights Act demands.

When the law can force a baker to make a cake, it can force a business to serve any customer at all. But owners should be able to serve the customers they wish. Although I am not gay, Jewish, black, or a videographer, I should not be required to do business with the Westboro Baptist Church, the KKK, skinheads, or a jihadist group. A tiny exemption for religion is entirely insufficient. The much larger principle is my freedom to associate as I see fit, leaving the marketplace and the court of public opinion to judge the commercial success of my choices.

Freedom from Religion

That freedom of association should extend to churches and marriages as well.

If government divorced itself from the religious aspect of marriage, churches could support marriage as they wished, free from government coercion to do anything they found offensive. If a church chose to sanctify only one-man-one-woman marriages, they would not be compelled to officiate for any other configurations. Other churches, voluntarily, would rise to proclaim their support for alternative marriages, while yet others would solemnize both. Church-goers would be free to attend whichever church—or none—that mirrored their values.

Such a system quietly extracts government from marriage, and, by removing so many accompanying barriers and mandates, provides actual choice for wedding couples.

But how do we answer the religious devotee who objects to that same-sex marriage, and to the forced cake baking, flower arranging, and picture taking that ensues?

We invoke freedom.

We acknowledge that the same freedom that prevents government from dictating the participants in a religious ceremony also prevents it from compelling service providers to serve that wedding.

This won't work if all sides aren't free to associate as they like. Ask Jack Phillips.

If same-sex marriage is legal, but everyone is forced to support (do business with) those marriages, we have freedom of association only for those getting married. If same-sex marriage is legal, and no one is forced to support it, then the freedom of association extends to everyone.

A consistent application of liberty can be difficult for those who want the government to support their traditional views. I understand that difficulty. Freedom is sometimes messy.

Freedom for everyone means that some people won't like what others do with their freedom.

Adlai Stevenson defined free society as "a society where it is safe to be unpopular." When we all exercise our freedoms, some mutual unpopularity is assured. So be it. I'd rather be unpopular than bullied by bureaucrats.

Of course, there are limits, even to freedom. Even religious freedom.

What stands in the way of a man who, under the guise of religious freedom, demands that his wives be kept as slaves? Supreme Court Justice Oliver Wendell Holmes said it colorfully: "The right to swing my fist ends where the other man's nose begins." A husband's freedom to act, regardless of justification, doesn't supersede anyone else's freedoms. No matter what his holy book says.

Freedom makes it safe to be unpopular, not uncivilized.

Anti-Political Solutions

So how can we acknowledge the very real cultural and historic traditions of marriage, while still respecting freedom of association in a modern society? Is it only government that can set the rules, or are there other possibilities?

Reframe the Questions

Proponents of historical and traditional marriage contend that same-sex marriage will undermine it. But traditional marriage is doing a pretty good job of that all by itself.

Divorce rates over the past century indicate that straight couples increasingly don't stay together, regardless of the existence of same-sex marriage. Though varying definitions make a single rate difficult to pin down, the most commonly cited statistic is that half of marriages end in divorce. The current rate for first marriages is perhaps half that, and higher for second and third marriages.

Is same-sex marriage the problem? Is the institution really so fragile that letting others in the club will break it more than it already has itself?

Notwithstanding the high divorce rate, traditionalists who press to maintain a one-man-one-woman structure for marriage commonly present arguments like these:

- Marriage has biblical roots, defined as between one man and one woman.
- The United States was founded by Christians, supporting Christian institutions.
- Same-sex couples cannot naturally procreate.
- Altering this definition of marriage will lead to further changes, such as polygamy.

Each point is debatable, but instead of bickering over them, what if we stipulate their validity for whoever cares to hold those views, and then reframe the question this way: Can the above points be both true to you and also none of the government's business?

Refuse to Be Puppets on Moneyed Strings

When government makes promoting marriage of a certain kind its business, moralistic and anticapitalist mischief ensues.

Our government fashions itself a benevolent and wise puppeteer, pulling our strings for the "greater good" of all. More marriage is good, Congress imagined in the 1940s, so it created the joint tax return to reward married couples. Too much concentrated wealth is bad, Congress later decreed, so it penalized married couples for making a high combined income. Such a legal and financial whipsaw treats citizens as puppets instead of individuals, encouraging otherwise self-sufficient citizens to cater to government whims in order to earn the tokens of government largesse.

Where marriage is concerned, I could use a good deal less of that type of benevolence and government wisdom. That same government wisdom allowed bans on interracial marriage until 1967. That same government benevolence discourages single mothers now from getting married.

When Lyndon Johnson's "War on Poverty" began in 1964, there was only one government assistance program that focused on helping single parents. Today there are dozens. Is the problem that much bigger, or has the government "solution" done the opposite of its intent?

To be sure, married couples are also eligible for many aid programs, but most of the money still goes to single parents and their children, and current policies perpetuate that. Women on welfare lose money when they marry. Couples also receive better Obamacare benefits when they stay unmarried. Incentives like these matter, leaving families worse off for it.

Nearly 80 percent of long-term child poverty occurs in broken or never-married families.

Even if it made sense to encourage marriage in the abstract, that should not be the government's purview in the particular. It's outside of government's role to provide incentives or disincentives for social experiments—especially given its track record of ruining nearly everything.

Form a More Perfect Union

According to the U.S. Census Bureau's "American Community Survey: 2012," more than 15 million unmarried partners live together. That number has increased tenfold between 1960 and 2000, with actual marriage rates falling by greater than 20 percentage points since the 1960s. Better than half of these unmarried couples marry within five years of moving in together, while 40% break up within that same time period. About 10% remain in an unmarried relationship for five years or more.

In light of these statistics, sources as diverse as The Heritage Foundation and the *New York Times Magazine* agree on the same idea: Children do better when their parents are married.

If marriage benefits families, creating happier, healthier, wealthier couples and better outcomes for children, and if the government is ill-equipped to encourage marriages, then who should?

Groups like The National Association for Relationship and Marriage Education (NARME) champion the cause using credible research. NARME knows that reversing the decline in marriage will lead to a healthier and more prosperous society. NARME is *for* people being in healthy relationships.

Julie Baumgardner, NARME's board chair, points to years of data on the topic. "Research for decades has shown that children do better when their parents are married as opposed to not being married. And this research holds even when unmarried parents are living together."

"What we know based on research is that couples do want to marry, but they don't want to go through the pain they saw their parents go through," Baumgardner adds. "They lack the confidence that they know how to make a marriage work over time. They just don't know the benefits they're missing out on."

Married couples are also statistically healthier and more financially secure than unmarried couples. The economic status is especially poignant for the children. "A child whose parents are married has only a 7% chance of growing up in poverty," Baumgardner says. "That number jumps to 40% for children whose parents aren't married."

Those who care to encourage and strengthen marriage, outside of the political process, can learn more at www.narme.org, where opportunities to donate and volunteer abound.

Be Like George Washington

For thousands of years, governments had no role in marriage. With churches the dominant cultural and economic institutions, there was no need. In America, even George Washington didn't have a government license to get married.

In the years since our government finally chose to intervene—and then only to stop interracial marriage—we've seen government despoil the institution. They ruin it by over-prescribing who can marry. They ruin it by capriciously exploiting their monopoly on licensing. They ruin it by overemphasizing its religious legacy. They ruin it by over-legislating commerce around the ceremony, and they ruin it by using the tax code to reward or punish certain family structures.

With that history, why do we place so much importance on government approval of any marriage?

In April 2015, Alabama Republican State Senator Greg Albritton offered a bill to separate the religious sanctity of matrimony once again from the civil contract of marriage. Senator Albritton's bill would have reduced the state's role to a mere acknowledgement of marriage, to be "recorded by the state after filing a simple contract between two people eligible to be married that is solemnized by a pastor, attorney, or other authorized witness."

Senator Albritton told the Associated Press:

> When you invite the state into those matters of personal or religious import, it creates difficulties. Go back long, long ago in a galaxy far, far away. Early 20th century, if you go back and look and try to find marriage licenses for your grandparents or great grandparents, you won't find it. What you will find instead is where people have come in and recorded when a marriage has occurred.

Although his bill was killed in committee, his approach holds promise that we might in time entertain the conversation on a larger scale.

Simplify Marriage

What we've done in America is conflate two distinct aspects of marriage, and in the confusion we've put too much authority where it doesn't belong.

Marriage is, by law, a contract. Ensuring that the contract is entered voluntarily, and validating signatories to that effect, is government's business. Recording the contract is government's business. Enforcing the contract, should it be necessary to dispose of assets or adjudicate child custody, is government's business. But that's as far as its reach should extend. Limiting who can perform a wedding ceremony, and which consenting adults can choose to marry? Not government's business. That's way too personal to leave to bureaucrats.

Beyond its legal elements, marriage is also a sacred promise, much more intimate than any government entity has the power to sanctify. That profoundly personal element, that avowal of love beyond measure and of hearts eternally united, demands private recognition based on personal choice. And it demands complete freedom in its celebration.

A simpler notion of marriage acknowledges these distinctions, separating the civil contract the government rightfully oversees from the cultural and social union that participants can enter into and commemorate as they choose.

With its authority properly restricted, government involvement does not intrude into a marriage process or celebration in any way. Participants decide for themselves whether to have a ceremony at all, and with whom—or with no one else at all. Perhaps it's religious, consecrated by their like-minded church or synagogue or mosque, officiated by their clergy, and held among throngs of well-wishers who share the participants' joy. Perhaps it's secular, or quietly alone on a beach.

But whatever the occasion, it's none of the government's business.

CHAPTER 11

IMAGINE CHOOSING

When voters demand a government that no longer controls every aspect of the Fireworks issues—schools, guns, marriage, and abortion—what does life look like day to day?

We Finally Understand What Government Can't Do

A different mindset arises. Americans look first to themselves and their communities to fix problems—not the government, because government's authority is limited to a defined set of functions: protect our rights, mediate disputes, and defend the nation.

That tiny list has no room on it for "fix all of society's ills." We look back to a time when we thought it could, and shake our heads at how little we learned every time we saw it fail to "fix" problems, only to return to government *despite that failure* and expect a different result.

We feel like someone who has finally left an abusive, lying spouse, and wonder why we ever tolerated such treatment.

Next generations listen to stories about how the government used to tell us what kind of light bulbs we could buy, which health insurance we had to carry, and which ways we could not defend ourselves. They are astonished that we ever let the government control us so completely.

Schools Fill Needs or Fail

With empowered consumers, how do schools compete for the business? The same way as Apple or Nike, by supplying what their customers want. Those that fail to do so simply fail.

Parents shop for schools like any other service.

Parents evaluate college readiness, safety records, SAT scores, and more. They consider their children's needs and find schools that have the right mix of music, art, math, science, vocational, and special-needs programs. More and more specialty schools arise in response to burgeoning market demand.

Graduation rates increase, because students are in environments matched to their interests and learning styles. Options abound: online, college-prep, traditional, STEM, classical, augmented home school, magnet, private, charter, and so many more. And when new teaching paradigms emerge (virtual reality, perhaps?), those options adapt to accommodate.

Without federal agencies controlling what must happen in schools, innovation thrives as schools race to deliver stronger results and better educate their students.

Even teacher quality increases, as the best qualified in every field are drawn to schools. The best chemists want to teach students who are excited to learn chemistry, and in return those teachers are paid market wages, free of government handcuffs on salaries and teaching methods.

Guns Are Practical Tools

Guns take their rightful place on the tool shelf, no more stigmatized than power drills. Society recognizes that areas with more gun ownership by law-abiding citizens deter those intent on using firearms for evil ends.

Families with a firearm in the home face no restrictions, and are the norm. Gun owners who use a firearm inappropriately face swift and certain justice, but very few do so, just as very few people intentionally run over people with their cars.

Schools regularly hold gun safety training, no different than drivers training classes. High schools and colleges sport competitive rifle teams, scouted by the USA Shooting Team for future Olympic hopefuls.

Law-abiding citizens are assumed armed; there are certainly no restrictions to the contrary.

*The first concern of criminals is inadvertently
confronting an armed citizen.*

Criminals have more incentive than ever to find a real job, as crime becomes too dangerous an option for them.

Abortion Is Rare

Americans acknowledge that *Roe v. Wade* is here to stay, and activists who want to reduce the number of abortions shift their focus. They no longer spend millions trying to make abortion illegal, as they have learned that such laws are more likely to increase than decrease the number of abortions. Instead, they champion private organizations that have been proven effective.

Because the economy is more free and open, women have far fewer abortions due to financial stressors. The number of abortions drops accordingly. Also, because so many adults have seen their own ultrasound when they themselves were *in utero*, people begin to look differently at what a life is.

*People may disagree on when life begins, but they begin to agree
that looking to the government for solutions to abortion never helps.*

The Benefits of Marriage Are Clear

Proponents of traditional marriage look for ways to support it while allowing for others to enter their own contracts, acknowledging that granting such freedom of association to everyone has important and far-reaching consequences. They appreciate marriage for all its benefits: longer life and health, greater wealth, and happier children. People who choose not to marry are neither chastised nor shamed, but those who choose marriage earn a reputation of being more savvy and successful.

*The government records marriage contracts,
but no longer controls marriage.*

Churches alone choose which marriages they sanctify, and face no criticism for any exclusions, as all people seeking to marry know they can find a church that matches their sentiments. And no business is forced to provide services for weddings they don't endorse.

We Quit Limiting Our Neighbors' Freedoms

We have become a culture that is not obliged to approve of everyone else's choices. If my neighbor worships the Flying Spaghetti Monster or celebrates Festivus, then so be it. When I don't like such a choice, I shrug my shoulders and move on with my own life.

My friend, writer Glenn Miller, said it best in his blog post "My Utopia Is Filled with Things I Despise":

> I don't much like guns and will probably never have one. In my utopia there are guns.
>
> I don't smoke—cigarettes, marijuana, doesn't matter. Not my thing, and kind of nasty. In my utopia people smoke.
>
> I don't have any use for a big church. In my utopia steeples litter the countryside.
>
> Big sugary drinks. Giant solar arrays. Trans fats. Caffeine. Cookie-cutter schools. One-size-fits-all healthcare plans. Which charity to support.
>
> Pick for yourself, but not for me. I certainly won't be picking for you.
>
> In my utopia I trust you.
>
> My utopia isn't filled with people just like me, nor with anybody who would want me to set the rules for what they should like. Neither I nor any dictator, no matter how benevolent, is wise enough to identify some universal good behavior—beyond leaving other people alone— and prescribe it for the rest of us.
>
> In my utopia you choose what you want to do and who to associate with. So do I.
>
> My utopia is filled with things I despise—and the choice to avoid them.

Our neighbors' actions might offend us, and ours might offend them, but we don't ask the government to make our neighbor more like us nor protect us from taking offense at ideas and actions we deplore.

Government Incentives Work

When government's authority is limited, we develop systems to roll back its previous excesses.

Government departments are incentivized to fix problems, not to increase the size of their next-year budgets. Agencies administering welfare and food stamps are rewarded for reducing the need for their services. Bonuses for city employee are based on reducing the time and cost to issue permits and licenses. State legislators are rewarded for reducing the tax burden every year.

And big, bloated government operations like the Department of Education, Federal Emergency Management Agency, and the U.S. Department of Agriculture have missions to put themselves out of business as soon as possible.

Incentives matter, both in the private and public sectors. We leverage that incentive engine, and use properly constructed rewards for government employees to promote prosperity for citizens and taxpayers.

Imagine the World Unencumbered

Imagine a world of self-control and prosperity.

Government focuses on keeping the peace and little else. Politicians, unburdened by micromanaging the behavior of free citizens, and without the distractions of social-issues Fireworks, maintain order better and buttress a strong and diverse marketplace.

As paternalistic laws and regulations vanish, amazing things start to happen.

Because government is much smaller, tax rates are lower, so individuals retain greater percentages of their income. More families can choose to keep a parent at home if they wish. A nice house no longer requires two salaries; a second income is icing on the cake.

Every decision you make is yours, along with all of its consequences. Jobs are plentiful because businesses no longer spend half of their day complying with government regulations. Instead, they are inventing, producing, and hiring. The marketplace thrives.

You trust that your prescriptions are safe because an independent company, similar to Underwriters Laboratory, stays in business by being precise about such things. Similar private organizations validate food and water quality.

A trip to the hardware store reveals a selection of bathroom fixtures of all prices and styles. Consumers select the fixture of their choice, knowing that they alone are responsible for the water bill.

Since a family's tax bill is so small, more remains in family budgets for churches and private charities. Donors evaluate what they give with as much scrutiny as they monitor their other consumer choices, remembering with amusement when money was taken from their paycheck for causes they may have denounced. Now they are prosperous enough to make a difference, and free to choose which organizations to support: pro-life or pro-choice, gun control or gun rights, school choice or public schools, traditional or same-sex marriage. With no tax dollars supporting these organizations, citizens feel a strong sense of ownership and satisfaction by privately supporting causes they endorse.

Schools compete for students, and offer customized options that match consumer demand. Even the worst schools in the new locally managed districts outperform schools from the old federally controlled system. Those that don't, close.

People take responsibility for their own lives. Neighbors help one another, but only voluntarily and from a joint sense of community. Very few people are financially dependent on others, and then only because of developmental or physical challenges. Most people are anxious to help them.

Children are happy—not because life is easy, but because they have learned to cope by overcoming the challenges of living in an unsheltered world. Because the government no longer bans so many things "for the children," those same children have earned authentic self-esteem and resilience.

Is our new country perfect? Of course not—utopia was never a choice in the real world.

But by not surrendering our problems to the government, by not abdicating our natural role as sovereign citizens, by owning our choices and their outcomes, we reclaim the vibrant and empowering humanity that centuries of serfdom have eroded.

Resources

If you care to learn more about some of the key ideas in *Government Ruins Nearly Everything*, you might find these resources to be of interest.

Former Libertarian Presidential candidate Harry Browne and his writings, especially *Why Government Doesn't Work*, available at harrybrowne.org.

Cam Edwards' web show on NRANews.com, for daily Second Amendment and nanny-state news and his book (co-authored with Jim Geraghty) *Heavy Lifting*.

Run Mitch, Run, by Don V. Cogman, for its idea of the "social issues truce."

Save the Storks (savethestorks.com) and other private pregnancy crisis centers.

Don't Shoot: One Man, a Street Fellowship, and the End of Violence in Inner-City America, by David M. Kennedy.

More Guns, Less Crime: Understanding Crime and Gun-Control Laws, by John R. Lott, Jr.

American Enterprise Institute (aei.org), for their many research papers and very helpful and gracious contributors.

Camp Compass Academy (campcompass.org).

Eddie Eagle GunSafe® Program (eddieeagle.nra.org).

National Alliance of Public Charter Schools (publiccharters.org) and National Charter School Resource Center (charterschoolcenter.org).

National Association for Relationship and Marriage Education (narme.org).

About the Author

L aura Carno is a Colorado citizen who understands that politicians are not kings, endowed with some birthright to parcel out our freedoms in tiny doses as they see fit. She knows it's not the job of hired civil servants to tell us what size soda to drink, what kind of insurance our family needs, or how we should best defend ourselves.

She believes instead that we're all adults who don't need to be told how to live, but who instead need to stand their ground when government gets the relationship with its citizens upside down. When elected officials forget whose money they are spending and whose rights they are eroding, when they forget who's the boss and who's the public servant—then it's up to citizens to speak out and reset the balance.

Find her speaking out against the "Mother, May I?" culture, one issue at a time, at www.lauracarno.com and @LauraCarno.